Container Gardening *for* Washington *and* Oregon

Marianne Binetti and Don Williamson

with Alison Beck and Laura Peters

LONE
PINE

Lone Pine Publishing International

The Distributor: Lone Pine Publishing
1808 B Street, Suite 140
Auburn, WA USA 98001
Website: www.lonepinepublishing.com

Publisher's Cataloging-In-Publication Data
(Prepared by The Donohue Group, Inc.)
Binetti, Marianne, 1956-
   Container gardening for Washington and Oregon / Marianne Binetti and Don Williamson ; with Alison Beck and Laura Peters.

   p. : ill. ; cm.

   Includes index.
   ISBN-13: 978-976-8200-41-9
   ISBN-10: 976-8200-41-3

1. Container gardening--Washington. 2. Container gardening--Oregon. I. Williamson, Don, 1962- II. Beck, Alison. III. Peters, Laura, 1968- IV. Title.

SB418 .B56 2008
635.9/8609797

Front cover photograph by Proven Winners

Every effort has been made to correctly identify photographers whose works are in this book. If we have erred, please let us know. All photos by Laura Peters except: AASelection 167b, 172b; Sandra Bit 28b, 51a, 150b; Conard-Pyle Roses 181b; Tamara Eder 58a&b, 59b, 97, 101, 116a&b, 125, 127b, 133a&b, 139a, 142, 151b, 157b, 160, 161, 174, 176, 182a&b, 186b, 192, 194, 209a, 220b&c, 223c; Jen Fafard 39b; Derek Fell 129b, 136, 180b; Erika Flatt 43; Janet Loughrey 128, 187; Heather Markham 16, 137; Tim Matheson 40a&b, 57a, 104, 105, 110b&c, 111, 112, 114a&b, 119, 120, 135b, 143, 151a, 157a&c, 163, 172a, 179, 191, 193a&b, 220a, 223a; Kim O'Leary 123, 129a; Allison Penko 127a, 139b, 149; Photos.com 57b, 204; Proven Winners 3a&c, 11, 17, 18b, 19a, 20a, 21a, 22b&c, 23b, 25a, 26a, 27a, 38b, 39a, 52b, 53a, 54b, 60a&b, 61, 96, 98, 106a&b, 108, 109, 126, 130, 134, 144, 153, 159, 162, 165, 169, 170, 175, 177, 184, 185, 188, 189a, 197, 199, 200, 203a, 205, 207, 223b; Robert Ritchie 59a, 180a; Nanette Samol 15b, 29a, 30a,b&c, 33b, 42, 44a&b, 45a,b&c, 46a,b,c&d, 47a, 48b, 56a&b; Peter Thompstone 158; Vincent Woo 14a, 15a; Tim Wood 107a,b&c, 110a, 118, 148, 209b.

This book is not intended as a 'how-to' guide for eating garden plants. No plant or plant extract should be consumed unless you are certain of its identity and toxicity and of your potential for allergic reactions.

PC:*P14*

Table of Contents

Preface

Think you don't have a green thumb? Been disappointed with your growing results? This book will help you contain all your garden problems.

Container gardening is the ultimate problem solver. If you have clay soil that drowns plants in our wet winters, those plants will survive in pots. Sandy soil near the coast often dries out too quickly, and root infested soil under large trees also causes gardening challenges that are solved when you garden in pots. No room in your condo for a vegetable garden? You can have a bountiful balcony by becoming a container-garden farmer. From the cool wet winters in western Washington and Oregon to the hot dry summers in the central and eastern parts of the states, you'll be able to contain your frustration, but not your enthusiasm, when you let your garden and your imagination go to pots.

The Pacific Northwest is blessed with not only a huge variety of plant material and independent nurseries that grow and sell quality stock, but also with access to excellent, inexpensive potting soils. Container gardens are only as good as the soil that is placed into them, and the easy access to the raw materials used in potting soils makes packaged potting soils available and economical at every nursery and garden center in our region. Good potting soil makes gardening in pots the easy answer to the most common growing problems.

Plants and potting soil are just two of the key ingredients for container gardening. The third component is the pot or container itself. The Pacific Ocean and the port cities along the coast bring to our area a vast selection of pottery from which to choose. The fired-clay pots from China, Thailand and Japan arrive in vast lots from huge ships and quickly find their way into local nurseries and garden centers. Many of these imported pots are frost resistant and can handle the winters in our climate without cracking. The abundance of wood products from our forests means that rustic-looking cedar containers are available as well. But you don't even need to buy a pot. Communities in Washington and Oregon are full of independent and creative people who can turn just about any receptacle into a container for growing plants—from recycled bathtubs to rusty colanders and metal tool boxes. These unique containers showcase the resourcefulness of our local people in award-winning home and show gardens.

Creativity is the reason this book was written. A team of garden writers has put together the images, planting suggestions and how-to information with the goal of giving container gardening a fresh twist. Our aim is not just to get you growing, but to unleash your inner artist as well. You'll see vegetables mixed with flowers, formal urns with topiary, new plant varieties and old-fashioned favorites that you may have never considered happily growing in pots.

People garden as a way to make their space more beautiful, to de-stress and to have fun. Gardening in containers makes it easier to achieve all these goals. Dig in!

The Plants at a Glance

Pictorial Guide in Alphabetical Order

African Daisy
p. 62

Agapanthus
p. 63

Angel's Trumpet
p. 65

Arborvitae
p. 66

Asparagus Fern
p. 69

Bacopa
p. 70

Basil
p. 71

Argyranthemum
p. 68

Bay Laurel
p. 72

Begonia
p. 73

Bidens
p. 75

Black-Eyed Susan
p. 76

Black-Eyed Susan Vine
p. 78

Blood Grass
p. 79

Blue Fescue
p. 80

Blue Oat Grass
p. 81

Bougainvillea
p. 82

Bugleweed
p. 83

Calla Lily
p. 84

Catch-Fly
p. 87

Cilantro • Coriander
p. 88

Canna Lily
p. 86

Clematis
p. 89

Cleome
p. 91

Clover
p. 92

Coleus
p. 93

Coral Bells
p. 95

Crocosmia
p. 97

Cuphea
p. 98

Dahlia
p. 99

Daylily
p. 101

Dogwood
p. 102

Dusty Miller
p. 104

Dwarf Morning Glory
p. 105

Elder
p. 106

Elephant Ears
p. 108

Euonymus
p. 109

Euphorbia
p. 111

False Cypress
p. 113

Fan Flower
p. 115

Flowering Maple
p. 116

Foamflower
p. 117

Fothergilla
p. 118

Fuchsia
p. 119

Geranium
p. 121

Golden Hakone Grass
p. 124

Golden Marguerite
p. 125

Hardy Geranium
p. 126

Glory Bush
p. 123

Hebe
p. 128

Heliotrope
p. 130

Hens and Chicks
p. 131

Hosta
p. 132

Hydrangea
p. 134

Hyssop
p. 136

Impatiens
p. 137

Iris
p. 138

Japanese Painted Fern
p. 140

Kalanchoe
p. 142

Lady's Mantle
p. 143

Lamium
p. 144

Lavender
p. 146

Lobelia
p. 150

Licorice Plant
p. 147

Lilac
p. 148

Lilyturf
p. 149

Lungwort
p. 153

Lotus Vine
p. 152

Lysimachia
p. 154

Maidenhair Fern
p. 155

Maple
p. 156

Million Bells
p. 158

Mondo Grass
p. 159

Monkey Flower
p. 160

Nasturtium
p. 161

Nemesia
p. 162

Nicotiana
p. 163

Oregano
p. 164

Oxalis
p. 165

Pansy
p. 166

Parsley
p. 168

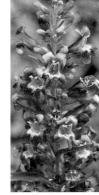

Penstemon
p. 169

Perilla
p. 170

Petunia
p. 171

Phormium
p. 173

Piggyback Plant
p. 174

Plectranthus
p. 175

Poor Man's Orchid
p. 176

Rhododendron·Azalea
p. 179

Rose
p. 181

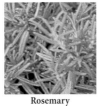

Rosemary
p. 183

Purple Fountain Grass
p. 177

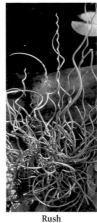

Salvia
p. 185

Scarlet Runner Bean
p. 187

Sedge
p. 188

Rush
p. 184

Sedum
p. 190

Serviceberry
p. 191

Snapdragon
p. 192

Snow-in-Summer
p. 194

Spider Plant
p. 195

Spruce
p. 196

Swan River Daisy
p. 197

Sweet Alyssum
p. 197

Sweet Flag
p. 199

Sweet Potato Vine
p. 200

Thyme
p. 202

Tradescantia
p. 203

Tulip
p. 204

Verbena
p. 205

Vinca
p. 206

Weigela
p. 207

Yarrow
p. 208

Yew
p. 209

Yucca
p. 210

Introduction

garden or a shaded woodland when pots of different shapes and sizes are filled with varied plant combinations to achieve a certain feel, look or environment. Even one large container can provide you with all the pleasure gardening has to offer.

Container gardening can be a benefit to people with limited mobility, such as the disabled and the elderly, who require easy access to their gardens. A garden with wide paths, raised beds and containers is ideal for able-bodied gardeners but even better for those who require the extra space for accessibility and stability. A stable, wide edge of a raised bed offers a seating area at a comfortable height for people who cannot work for extended periods while standing.

Container gardening is a wonderful way to enhance large gardens and landscapes. Containers expand the space available for growing plants, especially those plants that require specific growing conditions such as poor soil or a soil that is not typical for the area. Many

Container gardening is one of the most practical and flexible forms of gardening and is suitable for every level of gardening expertise, demographic and landscape, even if that landscape is only a balcony. Almost every plant that can be grown in a conventional garden can be grown on a smaller scale in a container. Container gardening is an excellent opportunity for gardeners who live in apartments, condominiums or small homes with only a patio or balcony to grow and nurture their own gardens. Gardeners can use containers to create theme gardens, grow vegetables, plant an orchard or grow flowers to pick for a vase or fresh herbs to add to favorite recipes. A small deck or patio can be transformed into a tropical oasis, an English cottage containers can be easily positioned to take advantage of light conditions not available in the regular planting areas of your garden or landscape, and containers with tender plants can be moved to areas where they are protected from the elements. Using containers as a physical barrier to confine plants with invasive tendencies allows you to grow these plants without having to contend with their spreading into unwanted places.

Container plants are used as focal points, set in places to draw your attention or to mark entrances such as doorways, sidewalks, driveways and garden paths. Beautifully planted containers can also be used to draw your eyes away from distracting items or areas you would prefer to remain unnoticed. Containers can be used to provide seasonal displays throughout the year, depending on the region. Containers can also be placed in beds and borders to fill gaps left by plants that finished blooming earlier in the season, were decimated by pests or disease, or were simply not performing as desired.

Containers are also great places to experiment with companion planting. Companion plants are those that form a symbiotic relationship when planted together, such as one plant providing protection from pests while the other plant provides nutrients needed by the first. Overall, this combination of plants may also improve the growing conditions by shading the roots or suppressing weed growth.

Container gardening can be a time and money saver. Many of the tedious chores such as weeding, lawn mowing, digging and raking are reduced or eliminated when you garden in containers. The use of automated watering systems or water-holding polymers and other materials, combined with slow-release fertilizers, can make your container garden a very low-maintenance affair. The smaller gardening area will also cost less than an average garden. You will have to make an initial investment in containers and a few tools and supplies, but your annual costs will include only plants, fertilizer and growing media. Once you become more proficient at growing plants in containers, you'll learn how to cut costs, as well as the overall amount of work involved, even further.

The only limits to what can be done with container gardening are the limits you place on yourself. Just let your imagination run wild, and remember that making mistakes is all part of the learning process. There is really no way to fail at gardening if you keep an open mind and just have fun experimenting. That's the beauty of container gardening— there's no long-term commitment. You can change your containers completely from one season to the next, regardless of what you've chosen to grow.

Vertical and Rooftop Gardening

Vertical Gardening

Vertical gardening is a method of gardening where a large number and variety of plants can be grown in a limited space, such as a balcony or patio. Vertical gardens can be used to block an ugly view or provide privacy. Vertical gardening also allows the disabled and elderly easier access for maintaining the plants and enjoying the garden.

Vertical gardening is as easy to do in containers as it is in a regular garden. Containers that can be used for vertical gardening include raised beds, planter boxes, hanging baskets and any containers that are sturdy and stable enough for the plants you intend to grow.

Plants can be trained to grow up trellises, fences, arbors and walls, using space that would otherwise remain empty. Vines and other natural climbers are great choices for growing on trellises and other structures. Some vines will naturally twine around a structure, some will attach themselves to the structure with tendrils, aerial rootlets or suction cups, and some will need to be attached to the structure with soft ties. You will need to ensure that the container and climbing structure are sturdy enough to handle the weight of the plant without tipping over, and that they will not blow over in a strong wind.

Plants can be grown in hanging baskets and allowed to trail and spill over the edge of the basket. Hanging baskets can be hung from any sturdy support, ranging from commercially available poles to house eaves to tree branches. Hanging baskets can be raised and lowered with a pulley system, which makes maintaining the baskets easier. A small block and tackle system allows for heavy containers to be raised and lowered with ease. Tie a knot in the pulley rope so that if the rope slips out of your hands, the container will not hit the ground. Ladders can be used to reach high baskets if a pulley system is not possible. Watering can be done with a hose-end watering wand designed to reach up and into hanging baskets.

If you are going to hang a basket from a tree branch, make sure the strap is wide enough that the branch is not damaged and it is strong enough to support the weight of the basket.

Plants can also be grown in a variety of specialized containers including multiple-opening containers, stackable containers and grow walls. We are all familiar with the terra-cotta strawberry/herb planter that has a large opening at the top and smaller openings around the sides. There are now many different styles of commercially available containers with multiple openings. Stackable containers allow far more plants to be grown in a small surface area than do regular containers and in-ground gardens. Growing walls are containers that have a vertical planting surface. One type of growing wall is a tall, flat, upright container that resembles a section of lattice fence with plants poking out of it. Another type is a wall constructed of custom-formed cinder blocks that provide planting pockets at regular intervals. A growing wall can stand alone or be incorporated as part of a building wall, fence or barrier. There are also retaining wall blocks that have pre-formed planting pockets in the design, so your whole retaining wall can be planted.

Some pest problems experienced in regular gardens are reduced or eliminated in a containerized vertical garden. Hanging baskets prevent crawling pests from reaching the plants. Also, the plants are more exposed to air, which reduces the incidence of many different diseases.

Your vertical container garden requires the same type of maintenance as a regular container garden, except that the plants may need to be watered more frequently. A layer of mulch will help retain moisture. There are a few other points to keep in mind when planning your vertical container garden. You will need to determine if it will be shading other plants, keeping in mind that the amount of shade will increase as the season progresses. Try to grow plants that will remain in easy reach for maintenance. If the plants you are growing are sun-loving plants, place the climbing structure on the north side of the plants. Do the reverse for shade-loving plants. Also, be aware of the direction of the prevailing wind, and face the plants into the wind so that the wind pushes the plants onto the structure.

Rooftop Gardening

Rooftop gardening is one of the latest trends in the horticultural arena. Rooftop gardens come in different forms, from a thick layer of soil over an impermeable membrane that covers most of the roof surface to a collection of various containers set on the roof. Rooftop container gardens reduce pest problems even further than on-ground container gardens because any pest that has to crawl or walk to find its host, such as a browsing deer, is out of luck. Vandalism and theft are practically eliminated as well. Rooftop gardens in large urban centers provide respite for birds and butterflies that might otherwise lack adequate food and shelter.

Container gardening is ideal for a rooftop setting, but you must make sure the roof is sturdy enough to handle the weight of the pots, plants, soil and water. A structural engineer will be needed to determine how much weight your roof can hold. You may be able to have your containers on the roof in spring, summer and fall but need to remove them if you get any appreciable snow cover. The roof might not take the weight of the containers and snow combined.

You will need to have a handy source of water for watering the plants. Be aware that there will be more sunlight and wind on the rooftop, and containers will need to be watered every day. You can incorporate water-holding polymers into the potting soil and mulches to keep the containers moist. It is a good idea to trap as much rainwater for use as possible. You do not want to be hauling buckets of water up to the roof to water the plants. Pots, plants, soil, and other supplies will also need to be transported to the rooftop.

Rooftop gardens extend the growing season, as rooftops tend to be a warmer and drier microclimate. However, winds at rooftop level can be strong enough to break trees and shred herbaceous plants. Sturdy windbreaks protect the plants from strong winds. Windbreaks will also provide some shade from intense afternoon sun and some privacy from the neighbors. Evergreen plants in containers need extra protection in winter, as the wind and sun can quickly desicate a plant. Some plants may be better adapted to rooftop culture than other plants. Heat-loving plants such as hens and chicks and herbs are drought tolerant and are therefore excellent choices for the rooftop.

A well-designed container provides interest in the garden (left). Group plants with the same needs together (above).

Container Design

A well-designed container or grouping of containers can look stunning with trailing plants cascading over the edges and colorful mounds of delicate flowers and interesting foliage filling the centers. Container gardening will allow you the opportunity to create any style possible to suit the environment, whether it's a traditional, eclectic, contemporary or industrial setting. This form of gardening also appeals to those who enjoy experimenting with combinations of plants until they discover the perfect arrangement, and to those who prefer to switch it up from year to year, following the trends. Gardening in all its incarnations should be fun and enjoyable, and container gardening is no exception.

Choosing what you like from what will grow well in the conditions of your growing space is one of the steps to planning any garden. Deciding how to combine these plants is another important step. Containers should be treated like small flowerbeds, and the same principles of design apply as with ground-based plantings. There are no hard and fast rules to container design, but the following suggestions may help determine what will grow successfully and what will appeal to the eye. Just remember that everyone is different, and what appeals to one person may not appeal to another. This is an opportunity for you to indulge yourself and make your own design choices.

Including a variety of flower shapes and at least three different foliage textures will add interest to your containers. Overall container garden designs look best with at least one strong, vertical element.

Try to group plants that have the same needs together, such as water-loving plants, shade-tolerant plants or drought-resistant plants. This will make it simpler to take care of each container and can help prevent problems with insects and diseases.

If you are combining several different types of plants in one container, generally keep the tallest ones in the middle or to the back of the container. Compact and trailing plants can be kept closer to the front or the edge of the container so that they are not lost visually. Robust trailing plants are good choices for the corners of square containers, where they have some extra room to spread. Careful planning allows for the best light to reach all plants, makes them all easy to see and enjoy and gives the containers an attractive, well-balanced appearance.

Combining several different types of plants together (above & below).

You can use tall, sun-loving plants to provide shade for other plants. A trellis covered with tall, fast-growing morning glories or scarlet runner beans will shade containers of impatiens or hostas.

There are other features you may want consider when planning your containers. You can choose plants that all flower at the same time or whose flowering times are staggered. Flower and foliage color are important considerations, as is the texture of the plants. Combining different features creates interest and contrast in your containers. Other design elements to be aware of include scale and proportion, shape, balance and repetition.

PROVEN WINNERS

Cool colors (above) are soothing. Color echoing with warm colors (below).

Color

Color is often the first thing we notice in a garden. It is easy to make a dramatic statement with color in container gardens because they are confined and right in front of you. Traditional ground-based gardens take more effort to create those dramatic effects.

Sometimes, knowing where to start is overwhelming. Take inspiration from home decorating and lifestyle magazines or anything else you see. Keep in mind that different colors have different effects on our senses. Cool colors, such as blue, purple and green, are soothing and can make small spaces seem bigger. Warm colors, such as red, orange and yellow, are more stimulating and appear to fill large spaces. White combines well with any color, and plants that bloom in white help to keep the garden from becoming a blurry, tangled mess.

People use color in their interior spaces to relax when at home. This formula can also be used outdoors, especially in small spaces. Green combinations can provide a refreshing feel to a space, while pinks and blues can invoke a romantic environment. Fiery yellows, oranges and reds will add a liveliness and warmth to even the largest, most imposing spaces, and bronze, brown and neutral tones can appear contemporary and classy.

There are a couple of aspects of color to be aware of when planning your containers: color echoing and color harmonies.

Color echoing is using one color, which can be of various hues and intensities, throughout the garden to produce unity and flow. This has the effect of making it easy for your eyes to flow from one part of the garden to the next without abrupt changes. It is wise to keep the color of your house, outbuildings and structures such as fences in mind when deciding what color or colors to use.

Color harmonies involve the color designs we use to plan our containers, and they are easy to understand with the use of a color wheel.

Monochromatic designs use one color that varies in hue and intensity, or colors very close to it on the color wheel. For example, a monochromatic planting of yellow may include yellow-green without disturbing the harmony of the planting.

Analogous color designs use colors that are next to each other on the wheel,

Using black and white in the garden.

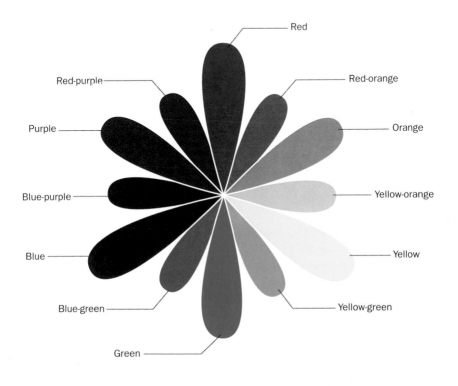

Red

Red-purple

Red-orange

Purple

Orange

Blue-purple

Yellow-orange

Blue

Yellow

Blue-green

Yellow-green

Green

Monochromatic (above). Complementary (below).

Analogous (above). Polychromatic (below).

such as blues with violets and greens. These colors add a little more spice to a design while maintaining the same mood of the planting.

Complementary color designs use colors that are opposite to each other on the color wheel. These combinations make bold and dramatic plantings that are hard not to notice.

Polychromatic color designs are those that most closely resemble the designs done by Mother Nature—a mixture of colors and textures seemingly tossed together in a haphazard manner. These can be some of the easiest designs to do.

There are now a number of plants available that come in very dark shades very close to black. The use of black, white and gray in planting designs helps make other colors really stand out, adds depth to small areas and plantings and helps tone down strong and complementary colors. A planting with all white flowers is a good choice for those whose gardening time is limited to twilight and evening hours.

Texture

Texture is an important consideration in container planting because different plant textures affect the perception of garden size and space. Some gardens have been designed solely on the basis of texture.

Foliage is the most important plant feature for achieving different textures in a planting. Large leaves are considered coarsely textured. Their visibility from a greater distance makes spaces seem smaller and more shaded. Small leaves, or those that are finely divided, are considered finely textured and create a sense of greater space and light. Textures, colors and size of foliage can vary greatly, creating a myriad of combinations.

Integrating textural foliage into a container design encourages people to get up close to touch the leaves. They'll want to determine whether foliage is rough, soft, spiky or smooth. Flowers come and go, but a container garden planned with careful attention to foliage, using a mix of coarse, medium and fine textures, will always be interesting.

Scale and Proportion

The scale and proportion of plants should match the size of the containers you plan to use. Large plants are used in large containers, and small plants are used in small containers. Large containers generally look best when they contain many plants, and small containers are best with a small number of plants. For container designs featuring a tall focal plant, the finished height should ideally be one to one-and-a-half times the height of the container. The exception to these guidelines would be for large specimen plants, which demand their own container, or at most have a fringe of trailing plants, and which often exceed the suggested plant-to-container height ratio.

The scale and proportion of the containers and plants should complement their surroundings. Often one large, well-planted container will look better in a small location than an array of smaller containers. Window boxes should match the style of the structure, and the planting should enhance the

The scale and proportion of your containers should match their surroundings.

A tall structural plant in a very tall container adds drama to a front yard.

space from both inside and outside the window. Too much height will block sunlight from the house, but some height in the middle of the box can be a nice touch. Trailing plants look best when they don't touch the ground.

Shape

It is important to choose plants with different shapes to provide variety in your container plantings. The careful use of shape can help add drama and emotion or tranquility and peacefulness. Imagine the silhouette of a city skyline and how dull it would look if all the buildings were square blocks of the same size. Tall, structural plants can be effective on their own, but they also work well as the main feature within a mixed arrangement. Rounded, billowy plants add bulk to a container planting. Short, trailing or mat-forming plants can soften the edges of containers and add depth, effectively increasing the diameter of the container.

Short, upright plants are great for filling open spots. Do not forget the shapes of the containers themselves. The shapes of your containers, when strategically placed and planted, can create stunning results.

Balance

Balance is easy to visualize by thinking of a scale, where what is on one side must balance with what is on the other side. In a design, balanced plantings are pleasing to the eye. There is symmetrical balance, such as one would see in a formal garden, where a line can be drawn up the center and one side is the mirror of the other, and asymmetrical balance, where the two sides are not the same but have the same visual effect. An example of asymmetrical balance would be a tall, narrow plant flanked by a mid-sized oval plant on one side and a shorter, wider plant on the opposite side. A radial planting has a central focal point with arms radiating out in all directions.

Radial symmetry is achieved when all arms are balanced.

Repetition

Repeating colors or shapes at intervals throughout the garden helps tie the whole design together. Repetition is a design element that is fundamental to many of the great gardens of the world. Whether this is done on a large or small scale, identical, repeated plantings can be used to emphasize or exaggerate perspective along a pathway, entrance or succession of steps. A row of identically planted pots can bring a sense of continuity to a space that seems chaotic and unbalanced, but it can also provide appeal to an empty space that begs for a simple focus. Placing a succession of large containers that stand above other in-ground plantings can create a stunning focal point.

Other Design Considerations

Grouping of Containers

Design principles also apply to the grouping and placement of the containers. With careful positioning, a group of varied and different containers can be arranged together for a greater impact. It is a good idea to move the containers slightly away from one another as the plants mature. This allows space in between the containers for the plants to fill and for the sun to reach the leaves.

Containers often look best when placed in a triangular outline. This can be a tall or large container in the middle with smaller pots on each side, or a tall container on one end with successively smaller containers sloping down to the other end. Formal placements often involve an *even* number of containers,

PROVEN WINNERS

such as a pair of square pots marking the front entrance of a house or two rows of containers forming an allée. Modern, eclectic and contemporary settings are best suited to repeated plantings with an *odd* number of containers as the focal point. A row of hanging plants looks best when all the containers are identical; however, the plantings do not need to be exactly the same. Cottage gardens, large rustic gardens with wild areas and other informal areas can benefit from a scattering of odd containers.

Adjusting the heights of the pots is another way to create a more luxurious display. Consider raising some of the containers on upturned pots, pot stands or shelves to offer further interest in your grouping.

PROVEN WINNERS

set, or one large container could have a number of scents within the easy reach of a comfortable chair. Container gardens lend themselves well to novelty themes, such as a salsa garden where the plants make up most the ingredients of your recipe, or a theme that integrates the pots into the design, such as different plant hairdos on pots with faces. Container gardening is also well suited to creating cameo gardens, which are small theme gardens in tucked-away places that are somewhat separated from the main garden.

Themes

Individual containers and groups of containers can be designed to follow any theme of your choosing—perhaps a Mediterranean theme, a native theme using plants that originate from your area or a tropical theme of plants that you fancy. A fragrance or aromatherapy garden full of herbs and scented flowers is great for accenting seating areas or for using in window boxes. Each container could contain a different scent, and the containers could be easily moved into place to enhance the mood you wish to

Desert-themed containers with cacti and succulents.

Creative Design Tips

Remember that anything that can hold soil and provide drainage is a potential container for creative gardeners. No need to contain your enthusiasm when you get creative with these container ideas:

• Pot up sedums and succulents in old leather shoes or boots. Nail cowboy boots to a wooden fence or hang a purse from a tree branch and pot up with trailing plants such as million bells.

• Metal wheelbarrows and wagons make great container gardens because they can be easily moved about for winter storage or to chase the sun. If metal containers are rusting out, line them with wire mesh and use rust preventative spray paint to restore them.

• Gardeners on the go might like to use old suitcases or footlockers to display potted plants. You can line old leather suitcases with plastic garbage bags, use a drill to add drainage holes and pot directly into the suitcase or metal footlocker.

• Need more space for more pots? Paint a ladder a bright color and place potted plants on the steps.

- Cracked and broken pots can still be put to good use. Lay broken pots on their sides half buried in the ground. Creeping plants like petunias can grow from the opening, and it will appear that the pot has fallen over and is spilling out the blooms.
- A trio of pots in three different sizes can be stacked and planted for a tower of flowers. Place an upside-down plastic nursery pot in the bottom of the largest pot and balance the medium sized pot on top of this. Fill in with soil around the base to help support the medium sized pot that is sitting inside the large pot. Repeat the process by placing the smallest pot inside the medium pot and using hanging plants around the sides. You'll have a pyramid of pots.

PROVEN WINNERS

Adding Accents to Your Potted Gardens

Container gardens don't have to be full of only pots. Early in the season, there are often spaces between young plants, and interesting accents can add personality and color while you wait for young plants to mature. Here are a few ideas:

- Polished stones or marbles add a bit of shine when used as mulch.
- Wine corks around the base of potted plants make a lightweight mulch and are especially festive around Mediterranean herbs such as basil, oregano and thyme.
- Chipped or cracked china plates or brightly colored plastic plates can be set upright and half buried into container gardens. This whimsical touch can be used to match the plates used on outdoor dining tables or just to provide a bold backdrop for blooming or trailing plants that spill over the container.
- Metal or stone remnants or architectural salvage can become the tall point or focal point of a large container garden. Imagine a slightly tilted stone pedestal or rusty metal bracket emerging from the center of a pot. Once the plants fill in around this accent, they'll have the "old world" look of a lost garden amidst the ruins.
- Mirrored gazing balls or glass orbs tucked into the soil around the plants will draw the eye to a container garden and help reflect the colors of the blooms.

The range and variety of containers is almost as plentiful as that of the plants you grow in them.

Container Selection

Containers range from fancy pots and urns of all sizes to wooden barrels, planter and window boxes, hanging baskets, washtubs and bathtubs, raised beds, galvanized metal buckets and even a pair of old boots. You can experiment with a number of different pots to see what works best. Anything that is sturdy enough to handle the weight of the plant and potting mix and will not fall over can be used as a container.

Bigger is better. A large container is less susceptible to fluctuations in temperature and requires less frequent watering. Large containers will provide protection to any bulbs, perennials, trees or shrubs you are going to over-winter. Choose containers that are at least 12" in height and in diameter. Smaller pots dry out very quickly, restrict the root area and reduce the plants' available resources. Deep-rooted plants will need deeper pots.

A screen will help prevent soil loss through the drainage holes.

Ensure that any container you use, regardless of the size, has adequate drainage. Drainage holes are either on the side of the container near the bottom, or on the bottom of the container. Containers can be set on bricks or commercially available "pot feet" to help with the drainage. If you don't want to purchase pot feet, you can slip small tiles or chipped tea cup saucers under the pots to raise them off the ground just a bit, making sure you don't block the drainage holes. Position these recycled pot feet so that they are hidden beneath the pot.

The drainage holes on the bottom of the pot will need to be covered with some material to prevent soil loss. Materials such as fine metal or plastic mesh, newspaper, weed barrier, broken clay flowerpot pieces (crocs), coffee filters and cheesecloth are suitable for covering the holes. Many container gardeners will add a 1–2" layer of coarse gravel over the screen to help improve drainage, but this is not totally necessary anymore, as today's plant mixes tend to drain very well. Using gravel, however, will help keep pots stable and will reduce the amount of planting mix needed in the container.

Light-colored containers are preferable to dark-colored ones, especially in sunny situations. They will reflect light

Unglazed terra-cotta pots (above) and glazed containers (right).

and will not heat up as much in the sun, especially in spring when overly warm soil can stimulate early plant growth that could be damaged by inclement weather. Preventing container heating also helps prevent roots from cheating or growing to one side of the container. Dark containers are ideal for design purposes because they provide a visual anchor like no other tone; just be cautious as to where and when you use them.

If you plan on moving your containers around, especially large, heavy containers, you may want to have them mounted on wheels. Heavy-duty drip trays, saucers and basic platforms are now available with wheels, allowing you to roll your containers around with relative ease. It's recommended that the wheels have a locking mechanism, but it's not always necessary.

Depending on where your container garden is, such as on a balcony, you may need to use drip trays or saucers underneath your containers. Saucers are useful in dry parts of the country because they help conserve water use. Saucers are most often made from clay or synthetic materials. Terra-cotta saucers retain moisture and may damage wood or painted surfaces.

Materials

Containers are constructed from a number of different materials including clay, metal, wood, stone and synthetics such as plastic and fiberglass. Be aware that some materials are more suitable for some parts of our climate than others.

Some materials are more appropriate for certain containers. Window boxes are usually made out of wood or plastic. Stone or metal is possible, but weight would be a critical determining factor. Wooden window boxes can also be custom built to blend in with the building architecture. Raised beds are built from wood, brick or stone and can also be designed to flow with the building architecture and existing landscape. Hanging baskets are often constructed of wood, plastic or wire, with weight again being a determining factor. There are a number of attractive stands available that provide sturdy support for hanging baskets.

Clay

Clay pots come in two basic forms, glazed and unglazed, in a plethora of shapes and sizes. Clay pots can be heavy, even when they are empty. They are subject to environmental conditions and can be damaged by cold weather. Clay pots will require special care, especially in areas that can freeze up fairly solidly in winter and areas that experience numerous freeze/thaw cycles.

Unglazed clay pots are often referred to as terra-cotta, which simply means "baked earth," referring to the kiln-firing process used in making the pots.

Terra-cotta containers are somewhat porous, which allows the plant roots to breathe easily but also allows for the quick evaporation of moisture, so they require frequent monitoring and watering. Terra-cotta holds heat into the night longer than wood, metal or synthetics. Be aware that terra-cotta containers also come in different qualities, and you often get what you pay for. Terra-cotta pots from Italy and other Mediterranean countries are usually very good quality. Terra-cotta ages beautifully over time like no other container material will. Within a few seasons, a combination of salts and organic growth will build on the walls of the pot, resulting in a lovely, natural patina.

Some gardeners do not like the look of salt build-up on the sides of their containers. You can renew the look of clay or terra-cotta pots by coating them with linseed oil. This helps remove the salt build-up and gives old pots a shiny patina.

Glazed clay containers offer another way to incorporate color into the overall design scheme of your garden. Glazed containers are not porous, so they will need a few drainage holes on or near the bottom. Glazed pots also benefit from a plastic lining, which helps prevent cracking if moisture seeps in.

Wood

Wooden containers are very adaptable and can be custom-built to fit into their surroundings. Wood offers more insulating value than clay, metal and stone, but it is susceptible to rot, so containers are often lined with plastic or coated with a non-toxic wood preservative. Some woods, such as cedar (*Arborvitae*), are relatively rot resistant. Do not use wood that has been treated with creosote or other toxic substances

Wood is great for building window boxes.

because they can emit compounds that can harm your plants. Wood is amiable to a variety of climates and can be used throughout our area. Make sure the containers are of sturdy construction. If you have wooden barrels, make sure the hoops and handles are firmly attached. To ensure the longevity of your wooden containers, particularly at the joints and seams, protect them with wood stain or wood oils, both of which enhance the natural grain and prevent cracking.

Linseed oil is the best oil to use to protect wood that is prone to drying out.

Stone

Stone includes terrazzo, concrete, reconstructed or refurbished stone and natural stone. Stone containers are available in a vast array of shapes, sizes, styles and colors. They tend to be quite heavy and difficult to move. It is best to plant stone containers after they are set in their relatively permanent location, unless they've been placed atop a strong platform or cart with wheels. Stone is often used to accent gardens, and aggregate planters allow stone to be seen on the container surface. Carved stone pots can be very expensive but will add a level of elegance to any formal container garden. A large rock with a trough makes a wonderful place for

tiny alpine plants but may need drainage holes drilled through the bottom. Stone containers are suitable for all of Washington and Oregon.

You can accelerate the aging process on the exterior of your stone containers by simply rubbing a fistful of fresh grass across the surface of the pot. The stain will quickly fade to brown. Brushing a thin layer of yogurt onto a pot's surface will encourage algae and lichens to grow, but a shady and moist location is necessary for the best result.

Metal

Metal containers can be made from tin, copper, bronze, iron, steel or lead and range in shape from simple buckets to fancy, ornate planters and urns. Be aware that metal pots absorb heat like dark-colored containers do. Most metal pots should be lined with plastic or protected from contact with the soil to prolong the longevity of the container, and make sure your metal containers have adequate drainage holes. To protect the drainage holes from rust, apply a coat of anti-rust paint. Plants in plastic containers can be inserted into decorative metal containers rather than using a lining.

Stone trough planter (left); a large aggregate container (right).

Synthetic containers come in all shapes and sizes.

To maintain the bright, reflective surfaces of your metal pots, use a soft cloth and window-cleaning spray. Do not use abrasive pads or cleaners. Be careful not to splash water or potting mix onto polished metal; the splashes may leave white calcium deposits, but they can be removed with a soft cloth.

Wire is used to make cage-like frames such as hanging baskets, planters and ornate plant stands that can double as planters. These frames are lined with sphagnum moss or some other suitable material before being planted.

Synthetic

The most commonly used synthetic materials for containers are plastic and fiberglass. These containers come in a vast range of shapes and sizes, from whimsical plastic duck and teddy bear planters to the newer fiberglass containers that resemble good-quality terra-cotta containers. Synthetic containers are not permeable, so they will need drainage holes. They are lightweight and easy to move with minimal concern for breakage, and most of them are good quality and inexpensive. Lower-quality plastic containers can deteriorate in the sunlight.

Synthetic containers are reliable containers for all climates and locations. Synthetic containers are a good choice for the apartment or condo dweller. They are lightweight and well suited for use on a balcony, and they can be easily moved back and forth seasonally.

Potting-mix stains, dirty handprints and general muck can be easily removed from most synthetic materials by simply using a soft cloth and soapy water. For tougher stains, a scouring pad may be necessary, but make sure to test a small, hidden area first in case the pad will damage the surface.

There are now spray paints made especially for plastic that make it easy to renew or refresh synthetic pots. Using matte black spray paint on any synthetic container will give it the look of a cast iron pot.

Container Gardening Environment

Sunlight

Where you choose to place your containers will determine the amount of sunlight they receive. Fortunately, many containers can be easily moved to accommodate the plant's need for more or less sunlight. Often the intensity of the sun can be amplified by the use of reflective materials around the containers.

Four levels of light may be present in your container garden: full sun, partial shade, light shade and full shade. Available light is affected by the position of the sun depending on the time of day and year, as well as by nearby buildings, trees, fences and other structures. Knowing what light is available in your garden will help you determine where to place your containers.

Full sun locations, such as along south-facing walls, receive direct sun for at least six hours a day. Locations classified as partial shade, such as east- or west-facing walls, receive direct morning or late-afternoon sun and shade for the rest of the day. Light shade locations receive shade for most or all of the day, but some sunlight does filter through to ground level. An example of a light-shade location is the ground under a small-leaved tree such as a birch. Full shade locations, such as under a dense tree canopy, receive no direct sunlight.

Sun-loving plants may become tall and straggly and flower poorly in too much shade. Shade-loving plants may get scorched leaves, or even wilt and die, if they get too much sun. Many plants tolerate a range of light conditions.

It is important to remember that the intensity of full sun can vary. For example, heat can become trapped and magnified between buildings, baking all but the most heat-tolerant plants. Conversely, a shaded, sheltered space that protects your heat-hating plants in the humid, hot summer may become a frost trap in winter, killing tender plants that should otherwise survive.

Exposure

Your garden is exposed to wind, heat, cold and rain, and some plants are better adapted than others to withstand the potential damage of these forces. Buildings, walls, fences, hills, hedges, trees and even tall perennials can reduce exposure.

Wind and heat are the most likely elements to cause damage to your plants, and cold can affect the survival of perennials, trees and shrubs. The sun can be very intense, and heat can rise quickly on a sunny afternoon, so only use plants that tolerate or even thrive in hot weather in the hot spots in your garden. Plants can be dehydrated in windy locations if they aren't able to draw water out of the soil fast enough to replace what is lost through the leaves. Tall, stiff-stemmed plants can be knocked over or broken by strong winds. Some plants that do not require staking in a sheltered location may need to be staked in a more exposed one. Temper the effect of the wind with hedges or trees. A solid wall creates wind turbulence on the downwind side, while a looser structure, such as a hedge,

A full sun location (above). A dark container in partial shade (below).

breaks up the force of the wind and protects a larger area.

All hanging baskets are particularly exposed to wind and heat. Water can evaporate from all sides of a moss basket, and in hot or windy locations, moisture can be depleted very quickly. Watch for wilting and water regularly. Wire baskets will hold up better in adverse

Hanging baskets are often very exposed to the environment.

conditions if you soak the moss or other liner in a commercially available wetting agent, which can be organic, and add some of the wetting agent to the water when first watering. Hanging baskets are a great place to add water-holding polymers to the planting mix.

One drop of a mild liquid dish detergent in one quart of water is a useful and cost-efficient wetting agent. The soap breaks down the surface tension of the water, which allows it to penetrate the material rather than just roll over the outer edge. This is helpful when you're unable to find wetting agents at your garden center.

Too much rain can damage some plants, as can overwatering. Established plants (or their flowers) can be destroyed by heavy rain. Most plants will recover, but some are slow to do so. Grow-covers are used to build temporary greenhouses, usually with a couple of wire hoops placed over the container and a

light, white fabric covering placed over the wires, which allows sun, air and moisture in and keeps bugs, birds and wet weather out. For exposed sites, choose plants or varieties that are quick to recover from rain damage. Many of the small-flowered petunia varieties and new petunia cultivars available recover well from the effects of heavy rain.

Frost Dates and Hardiness Zones

Depending on the types of plants you choose to grow and the types of containers you have, you will need to be aware of frost dates and hardiness zones. Many plants are hardy enough to survive winter outdoors in a large enough container, and many others grow to a mature size in a single season.

When planting annuals, consider their ability to tolerate an unexpected frost. Last-frost and first-frost dates vary greatly from year to year and region to region.

They can also vary considerably within each region. Consult your local garden center for more specific information.

Annuals are grouped into three categories based on how tolerant they are of cold weather: hardy, half-hardy or tender.

Hardy annuals tolerate low temperatures and even frost. They can be placed in your containers early in the year and may continue to flower long into fall or even winter. Many hardy annuals can be seeded directly into containers before

AVERAGE ANNUAL MINIMUM TEMPERATURE

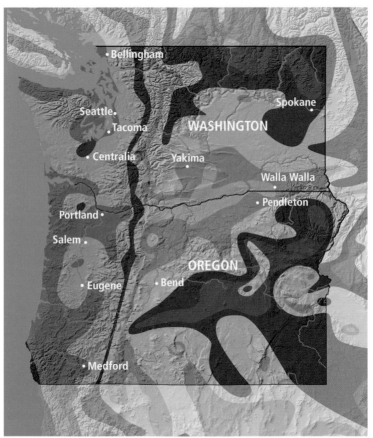

TEMPERATURE (°C)	ZONE	TEMPERATURE (°F)		TEMPERATURE (°C)	ZONE	TEMPERATURE (°F)
−28.9 to −31.6	4b	−20 to −25		−15.1 to −17.7	7a	5 to 0
−26.2 to −28.8	5a	−15 to −20		−12.3 to −15.0	7b	10 to 5
−23.4 to −26.1	5b	−10 to −15		−9.5 to −12.2	8a	15 to 10
−20.6 to −23.3	6a	−5 to −10		−6.7 to −9.4	8b	20 to 15
−17.8 to −20.5	6b	0 to −5		−3.9 to −6.6	9a	25 to 20
				−1.2 to −3.8	9b	30 to 25

Trees and stairwells can create a microclimate for your containers.

a chance to warm up. These annuals often have the advantage of tolerating hot summer temperatures.

Perennials, bulbs, trees and shrubs have a minimum temperature for survival and will have a hardiness zone designation. These plants will die if they experience a prolonged spell of colder weather. The USDA created the hardiness zone map based on minimum average winter temperatures and plant survival data. Many plants also have a maximum temperature threshold, above which they may die. Our area has a wide range of hardiness zones, and you will need to know the hardiness zone of your area. If you're not sure, ask at your local nursery or a savvy gardener friend.

Don't feel intimidated or limited by the information you find on hardiness zones. The divisions are based mostly on the average lowest winter temperatures. Mild or harsh winters, heavy or light snow cover, fall care and the overall health of the plants that you grow all influence their ability to live through winter.

the last spring frost date. Half-hardy annuals can tolerate a light frost but will be killed by a heavy one. These annuals can be planted into your containers around the last-frost date and will generally benefit from being started early from seed indoors, such as those transplants available from garden centers. Tender annuals have no frost tolerance at all and might suffer if the temperature drops to even just a few degrees above freezing. These plants are often started early indoors and are not planted in the garden until the last-frost date has passed and the ground has had

As well, local topography in the garden creates microclimates—small areas that may be more or less favorable for growing different plants. Microclimates may be created, for example, in the shelter of a nearby building or a stand of evergreen trees, in a low, still hollow or the top of a barren, windswept hill, or near a large body of water. Microclimates can raise the zone a notch and allow gardeners the possibility of growing a plant that everyone says won't grow in a particular area. Container gardening with plants that are borderline hardy is a challenging and fun part of gardening. Always continue to experiment and explore.

Perennials and shrubs for sale.

Container Principles

Choosing Healthy Plants

Many gardeners consider the trip to the local garden center to choose their plants an important rite of spring. Others consider starting their own plants from seed one of the most rewarding aspects of gardening. Both methods have benefits, and many gardeners use a combination of the two.

Purchasing plants is usually easier than starting from seed and provides you with plants that are well grown and often already in bloom. Starting seeds can be fun but a little impractical at times. It requires space, facilities and time. Some seeds require specific conditions difficult to achieve in a house, or they have erratic germination rates. Other seeds are easy and inexpensive to start. As well, starting from seed offers you a greater selection because seed catalogues have many more plants available than what are offered at most garden centers.

Purchased plants are grown in a variety of containers. Regardless of the size or age of the plant you're considering purchasing, most plants get established and grow quickly once they are planted in your containers. Most plants are sold in individual pots and in divided cell-packs. Each type has its advantages and disadvantages.

Plants in individual pots are usually well established, having been nurtured along in the nursery, and have plenty of

The plant on the right is much healthier than the plant on the left (above). A root-bound rootball (below).

space for root growth. The cost of labor, pots and soil can be expensive if you are purchasing a large number of plants. If you are planting a large container garden, you may also find it difficult to transport large numbers of these plants home. Potted plants come in many sizes.

Annuals, biennials and perennials grown in cell-packs are often inexpensive and hold several plants, making them easy to transport. These annuals suffer minimal root damage when transplanted, but because each cell is quite small, plants may become rootbound quickly and should be planted soon after you've purchased them. Although smaller plants are more economical in the long run, it will take

them longer to fill the container. For those of us who reside in a region with a short growing season, this may not work because the containers may not be full and lush until late into the year.

It is usually best to purchase plants that haven't yet flowered, but this isn't always a possibility, as many plants are strategically grown to be flowering as early as possible for the garden centers. Plants that haven't yet flowered are younger and less likely to be rootbound. Plants covered with an abundance of flowers or flower buds have already passed through a significant portion of their rooting stage, and while they will add instant color when planted, they will not perform at their best in the heat of summer, and their longevity can be compromised. Now this is not to say that you shouldn't consider blooming plants for your containers, but if you choose to buy annuals or perennials already in bloom, pinch off the blooms and buds just prior to planting. This encourages new root growth and a bigger show of flowers throughout the season.

Check for roots emerging from the holes at the bottom of the cells, or gently remove the plant from the container to look at the roots. An overabundance of roots means that the plant is too mature for the container, especially if the roots wrapped around the inside of the container resemble a thick web. Such plants are slow to establish once they are transplanted into the garden. Healthy roots will appear almost white. Avoid potted plants with very dark, spongy roots that pull away with little effort.

Plants should be compact and have good color. Healthy leaves look firm and vibrant. Unhealthy leaves may be discolored, chewed or wilted. Tall, leggy plants have likely been deprived of light. Check carefully for diseases and insects. Do not purchase a diseased plant. If you find insects on the plant, you may not want to purchase it unless you are willing to cope with the insects you are transporting home. To avoid spreading insect pests and diseases, deal with any problems with the plant before you transplant it into your garden.

Once you get your plants home, water them if they are dry. Plants growing in small containers may require watering more than once a day. Keep them in a lightly shaded location until you plant them. Remove any damaged growth.

Get your plants from a reputable source, especially trees, shrubs and perennials. Locally sourced plants will survive in your area better than plants imported form another state or country. Garden centers, mail-order catalogs, friends, family and neighbors are other sources for plants. A number of garden societies promote the exchange of plants and seeds, and many public gardens sell seeds of rare plants. Gardening clubs are also a great source for rare and unusual plants.

Staff at nurseries and garden centers should be able to answer questions, make recommendations and assist you with whatever you need. It will be helpful to them if you bring an overhead sketch of the area where you intend to have your container garden and mark potential locations of the containers. Be sure to mark shaded areas, windy areas,

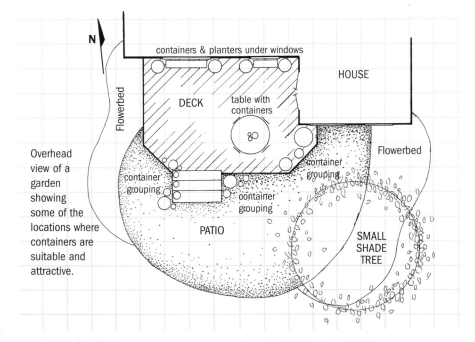

N

containers & planters under windows

HOUSE

Flowerbed

DECK

table with containers

Overhead view of a garden showing some of the locations where containers are suitable and attractive.

container grouping

container grouping

container grouping

Flowerbed

PATIO

SMALL SHADE TREE

with a knife or other appropriate scraping tool. Soak the scrubbed container in clean water for 15 minutes to remove the bleach and then give it a quick spray rinse. If you are cleaning glazed containers, make sure the glaze will not be damaged by the bleach.

Container Drainage

If your container does not have adequate drainage, you run the risk of drowning your plants. Some form of opening in the bottom of containers is essential for good drainage. Extra holes may need to be made in some containers that do not drain as quickly as needed.

Containers that have no drainage, or very minimal drainage, can be used to grow plants that do well in boggy conditions, such as those found along stream banks, ponds and other water features.

Decorative containers can be used just as they would indoors, where a planted pot is set into a decorative pot. Ensure that water is never allowed to collect or pool between the two pots; otherwise, the rootball will become waterlogged and begin to rot. This arrangement is only recommended for smaller containers.

garden and structure orientation (north, south, etc.) and so forth on the sketch, so that the professionals can help you choose appropriate plants. You will also find it convenient to take this book to the nursery. You'll have information about the plants and photos of them at your fingertips as you browse.

Preparing Containers for Planting

Container Cleaning

Starting with a clean container is important for minimizing soil-borne plant diseases and for removing deposits from fertilizers and plant root compounds released by the plant into the surrounding soil. Even new containers should be cleaned to remove any dust from transport and handling. Most containers are easily cleaned with mild soap and water with a good rinsing.

Terra-cotta pots require a different cleaning process. Soak the containers overnight or longer in a solution of nine parts water to one part bleach. Soaking the containers for a longer period of time makes the pots easier to clean. Use a wire or stiff-bristle plastic brush to give the inside of the container a good scrubbing. Deposits can be scraped off

Choosing a Planting Mix

Many plants need soil that allows excess water to drain away but still retains enough water and nutrients for the plants to use. Commercially available container planting mixes allow good drainage, are lighter in weight than garden soils, have nutrient-holding capacity and do not have soil-borne diseases or weed seeds. Avoid using garden soil because it drains poorly and tends to dry into a solid mass. A small amount

A selection of planting mixes

of good garden soil can be mixed into the planting mix, which adds minerals and microorganisms and improves the nutrient holding capacity but may also introduce soil-borne diseases. There are a variety of mixes available, depending on what properties your soil needs to have for the plants you want to grow.

Many commercial planting mixes now contain compost in varying percentages. High-quality compost should be an integral part of every container planting mix. Commercial mixes are also available with water-holding polymers already mixed in.

Regular commercial planting mixes are mainly peat moss or coir fiber and can contain tree bark, vermiculite, perlite, dolomite lime, sterilized loam or clay, superphosphate for quick rooting and often some form of slow-release fertilizer. Coir fiber is made from the husks of coconuts. It is more environmentally friendly than peat moss but can be harder to handle. Commercially available organic plant mixes are available in different formulations depending on what the manufacturer chooses to use in the product. They are mainly peat moss or coir fiber and may contain high-quality compost, composted leaf mold, bone meal, blood meal, humus, earthworm castings, bird or bat guano, glacial rock dust, dolomite lime, pulverized oyster shells, alfalfa meal, rock phosphate, greensand, kelp meal and beneficial mycorrhizal fungi.

If you plan on having a large number of containers, there are large bags and bales of commercial planting mix available. You can also make your own from bulk ingredients to reduce your costs. For the mix we suggest using 40% sphagnum peat moss or coir, 40% high-quality compost, 10% garden loam and 10% washed and screened coarse, angular sand. You can add in high-phosphorous guano or bone meal for a root booster, or you can mix in a commercially formulated organic fertilizer. For those plants that require an alkaline soil, dolomite lime or oyster shells can be mixed in to raise the pH. Add these fertilizer products as instructed on the label for the volume of soil your containers will use. A soil test is a useful tool for determining what additions and adjustments your planting mix might need.

Reducing the Weight of Your Containers

Containers can be heavy and steps can be taken to reduce the weight of your containers. Do not use gravel in the bottom of the containers and do not use planting mixes that contain soil or sand. If you will only be planting annuals in larger containers, some of the planting mix in the bottom half can be replaced. You can add in Styrofoam packing peanuts, broken pieces of Styrofoam packing from goods such as electronic products, well-crushed pieces of newspaper or shredded leaves, or you can use flipped over plastic pots set in place before the planting mix is added. Perennials and shrubs, however, may need all the container space filled with soil for roots to grow in.

Planting Your Containers

Generally, you can transplant into containers at the same time you would in a regular garden. There is a proper order to plant into containers. For plants, it is trees first, then shrubs, bulbs, perennials and finally annuals. For size, the largest plants go in first and work down in size to the smallest plants.

Terra-cotta pots should be soaked before planting. Given its porosity, the clay will draw the moisture out of the soil and away from your new plants.

Fill your cleaned container with moistened planting mix until it is approximately 75% full. Place the plants into their respective positions before even removing them from the nursery pots to check your arrangement. Once you've chosen where they're to go, begin working from the middle of the display outward to the pot's edge.

A selection of plants for a new container (top). Place mesh screen over drainage holes (bottom).

After removing the plants from the pots, gently tease the outside of the rootballs apart, or if the plant is rootbound, score the outer roots with a sharp knife to encourage the roots to spread out rather than continuing to coil into a mass.

Install trellises, stakes or other supports that are needed. Place the larger, central focal plants into the container first, followed by the smaller ones. Add more potting mix, as necessary, to surround the rootballs of the plants. Add the smallest and outer-edge plants last and top-up the potting mix, allowing at least 2" from the top edge of the pot for watering and perhaps a layer of decorative mulch. Ensure the planting mix is without gaps or air pockets in between or under any of the plants. This can be done by gently tapping the bottom of the pot on the ground or by slipping your hand into the potting mix to move the soil into gaps and pockets. Watering will also encourage the potting mix to settle without having to firm it down with your hands. Water until the container is thoroughly soaked. Add more planting mix if it settles too much after the first soaking.

Fill the container with an appropriate amount of planting mix (above). Place potted plants in the container to check placement (center).

Don't plant too deeply or too shallowly. Use the depth at which the plants are already growing as a guide for how deeply they should be planted. You don't want to have exposed roots above soil level, but you don't want to bury the crowns, which can lead to rot. If you're adding seeds to the mix, do so at this stage, planting at the depth recommended on the package.

Remove plants from their pots and deal with any excess roots (below).

How many plants to include in a container is a matter of preference, but overplanted containers look better than sparsely planted ones. This does not apply to specimen plants in their own containers. The spacing between plants in containers can be reduced from what is noted on the plant tag. However, too many plants in one container will be forced to compete with each other for space, water, nutrients and light, so you will still need some soil between each

Tease out some of the roots on the bottom of the root ball (top & center left). Make sure each plant has enough room (bottom). Water the freshly planted container immediately (center right).

plant to provide room for their roots to spread. Be aware that with more plants in a container, you will have to apply more water and fertilizer.

Water plants regularly when they are first planted. Containers can dry out quickly, and plants need to become established before they can tolerate adverse conditions.

We encourage you to make detailed notes and planting diagrams for each container, including when the container was planted and the common and scientific name of each plant for future reference. This is especially helpful when you want to replicate or avoid what you planted from one year to the next, based on your successes and failures.

Planting Trees and Specimen Plants

Ensure that the container is of sufficient size to allow for root growth, and include enough planting mix to insulate the roots and crown from extreme climate conditions. Planting mixes for trees benefit from having garden loam as part of the mix. This makes the container more stable and gives the tree something a little more solid to root into.

Most plants, especially trees, shrubs and perennials, should be planted in spring to early summer to allow them enough time to become established before facing a cold winter. This is, of course, if you want to overwinter the hardy plants in the containers. Some gardeners prefer to keep the hardier plants in the containers only for the growing season with plans to plant them in the ground later on. Others simply treat these plants as annuals rather than overwinter them.

Container Garden Maintenance

Your container garden will need regular maintenance just like regular gardens, but on a much-reduced scale. The most important tasks are watering and feeding. Weeding, grooming, relieving soil compaction and repotting are other tasks that require some attention. You will need a minimal selection of quality tools including a hand trowel, a hand cultivator, a watering can with a diffuser and by-pass hand pruners.

Watering

Watering is the most important maintenance task you will perform. Watering cans or buckets are good if you have only a small number of containers. Rainbarrels are great places to fill watering cans and buckets. Watering cans come with a diffuser that turns the water flow into a gentle rain shower, which helps minimize soil compaction. A hose with a watering wand is effective for a larger number of containers. Both of these methods are time consuming, but allow you to visit and inspect your containers regularly. You can use commercially available water-holding polymers, which are mixed into the planting

Organic amendments (left to right): moisture-holding granules, earthworm castings, glacial dust, mycorrhizae, bat guano, compost, bone meal and coir fibre.

Water until it drains freely out the drainage holes.

mix and act as a moisture reservoir, to reduce your watering time and cost.

Containers will need to be watered more frequently than plants growing in the ground. The smaller the container, the more often the plants will need watering. Containers, especially hanging baskets and terra-cotta containers, may need to be watered twice daily during hot, sunny and/or windy weather. Water until the entire planting mix is thoroughly soaked and water runs out of the drainage holes. To check if the container needs water, first feel the surface. If it is dry, poke your finger a couple of inches into the planting mix. If it still feels dry, it is time to water. You can also lift the container off the ground a little, and if it feels light, it probably needs to be watered.

If the soil in your container dries out, you will have to water several times to make sure water is absorbed throughout the planting medium. A good

method is to place the whole container in a bucket of water until the surface of the planting mix feels moist.

To save time, money and water, or if you plan to be away from your garden for an extended period, consider installing a drip irrigation system. Drip irrigation systems apply water in a slow, steady trickle, which takes somewhat longer than watering with a watering can or hose but still thoroughly soaks the containers. Drip irrigation reduces the amount of water lost to evaporation. Systems can be fully automated with timers and moisture sensors. Consult with your local garden center or irrigation professionals for more information.

You can lower your watering requirements by adding a thin layer of mulch to each container. You can also group containers together to aid in the reduction of evaporation from each container. Placing containers in sheltered locations can also reduce evaporation.

Feeding

Plants in containers have limited access to nutrients. Your plants may need a boost during the growing season, and you will have to apply some form of fertilizer. Plants that are heavy feeders will definitely need additional supplements. Commercially available fertilizer comes in various forms including liquids, water-soluble powders, slow-release granules or pellets and bulk materials such as compost. Follow the package directions carefully because using too much fertilizer can kill your plants by burning their roots. If you use a good-quality planting mix that has compost and an organic or slow-release fertilizer mixed in, you may not need to add extra fertilizer.

Many plants will flower most profusely if they have access to enough nutrients. Some gardeners fertilize hanging baskets and container gardens every time they water, using a very diluted fertilizer so as not to burn the roots. Too much fertilizer stimulates excessive plant growth and can result in lanky stems and weak or overly lush plant growth that is susceptible to pest and disease problems. Some plants, such as nasturtiums, grow better without fertilizer and may produce few or no flowers when fertilized excessively.

Healthy soil allows plants to grow better over the course of summer. Organic fertilizers enhance the micro-organism population in the planting mix, which in turn makes more nutrients available to the plants. Organic fertilizers don't work as quickly as many inorganic fertilizers, but they often don't leach out as quickly. They can be watered into planting mix or used as a foliar spray as often as weekly.

Organic fertilizers can be simple or complex formulations. They may include alfalfa pellets, well-composted animal manure, crab meal, coconut meal, corn gluten, kelp meal, sunflower meal, rock phosphate, humus, leaf mold, bone meal, blood meal, earthworm castings, bird or bat guano, dolomite lime, pulverized oyster shells, glacial rock dust, greensand and beneficial mycorrhizal

Pinching off a spent bloom.

fungi. Be aware that bone meal, fish emulsion and other odorous organic fertilizers may attract unwanted garden visitors that can cause major destruction.

Containerized trees and shrubs benefit from annually removing some of the planting mix from the container and topping it up with fresh, good-quality compost.

Weeding

Weeding your containers is easiest when the weeds are small. Well-planted containers often exclude enough sunlight to suppress weed growth. Also, don't forget about the weeds that pop up around your containers.

Grooming

Good grooming helps keep your container plants healthy and neat, makes them flower more profusely and helps prevent many pest and disease problems. Grooming may include pinching, trimming, staking, deadheading, training vines and climbing plants and pruning trees and shrubs.

Don't be afraid to trim any plant that is exceeding its boundaries (above).

Pinching refers to removing by hand, or with scissors, any straggly growth and the tips of leggy plants. Plants in cell-packs may develop tall and straggly growth in an attempt to get light. Pinch back the long growth when transplanting to encourage bushier growth.

Remove any yellow or dying leaves. Pinch back excess growth from more robust plants if they are overwhelming their less vigorous container mates. Keep trailing stems from touching the ground.

If annuals appear tired and withered by mid-summer, try trimming them back to encourage a second bloom. Mounding or low-growing annuals, such as petunias, respond well to trimming. Use garden shears and trim back a quarter to half of the plant growth. New growth will sprout, along with a second flush of flowers. Give the plants a light fertilizing as well at this time.

Some plants have very tall growth and cannot be pinched or trimmed. Instead, remove the main shoot after it blooms, and side shoots may develop.

Tall plants may require staking. Tie plants loosely to tall, thin stakes with soft ties that won't cut into the plant. Narrow ties are less visible. Stake bushy plants with twiggy branches. Insert the twigs into the planting mix near the plant when it is small, and as the plant grows it will hide the twigs. A careful selection of twiggy branches can add another attractive dimension to your containers.

Vines in containers can be used as trailers or trained to climb up trellises, netting or other structures. These are either inserted into the container, or the container is placed near the structure. Vines with tendrils climb best on structures that are small enough in diameter for their tendrils to easily wrap around, such as a cage-like trellis or netting. Other climbers will need to be woven through or tied to their structures. Do not be afraid to clip off any rampant or out-of-bounds growth.

Learn proper pruning techniques before trimming trees and shrubs.

Many annuals and perennials benefit from deadheading (removing faded flowers), which often helps prolong their bloom. Deadheading keeps the plants and your containers looking their best and prevents your containers from becoming a seed bank. Decaying flowers can harbor pests and diseases, so it is a good habit to pick off spent flowers when you are checking your containers. Some plants, such as impatiens and wax begonias, are self-cleaning or self-grooming, meaning that they drop their faded blossoms on their own. Leaving the seedheads on some plants, such as ornamental grasses, can provide winter interest.

Trees and shrubs will need to be pruned to keep them healthy and in proportion to the container. Each tree or shrub will have its own pruning requirements, such as the best time to prune and how much of the tree or shrub can be safely removed. It is important to learn where, when and how to make proper pruning cuts. There are books available that describe proper pruning techniques, and classes on pruning are available from horticultural college and university extension programs and public gardens.

Relieving Soil Compaction

Planting mixes in containers can experience soil compaction from the effects of constant watering. A hardened crust can form on the surface that does

Trees, shrubs and perennials will eventually outgrow their containers.

The top growth (leaves, twigs and branches) of trees and shrubs produces hormones that stimulate root growth, and the roots produce hormones that stimulate top growth.

not allow water and air to penetrate into the planting mix, which can be easily broken up with a good hand cultivator. Replace the top layer of planting mix annually in spring.

Repotting Plants

Trees, shrubs and perennials can stay in containers for a number of years with proper care and maintenance. At some point, the plants will become rootbound in their containers and will need repotting. Perennials should be divided at this time, and trees and shrubs will need their roots pruned.

Perennials need dividing when flowering is diminished, when the plant loses vigor, when the center of the plant has died out or when the plant encroaches on the other plants in the container. Replant perennial divisions as soon as possible. Extra divisions can be spread around into other containers, shared with friends or composted. Trees and shrubs that need repotting will also appear less vigorous and have reduced flowering.

The rule of thumb for choosing new containers is to use the next larger size. Perennials will be divided, so they may not need a larger container. Trees and shrubs will require containers only a couple of inches wider and deeper than

their current containers, and they will need some root pruning. Using too large a container can cause overwatering problems.

Tree and shrub containers can be heavy, and you may need help to tip the container over. You may want to wrap the branches in a blanket to prevent damage to the plant before you tip the container over. Gently remove the plant from the container and shake out some of the old planting mix. Tease out the larger roots that are encircling the container or growing in toward the center of the root mass and cut them off where they would have just touched the edges of the previous container. When tree roots are pruned or damaged, the plant responds by reducing its top growth. Allow the plants to do this naturally; wait and then prune off the dead branches when they become visible rather than pruning immediately. Replant the tree or shrub into its new home with fresh planting mix, ensuring it is firmly settled with no air pockets.

Containers with small openings might not allow freezing soil to expand.

Terra-cotta pots are subject to frost and cold damage.

Protecting Containers and Plants

Insulating Containers

Some plants prefer a cool, moist root environment during the heat of summer and some plants need extra protection from the effects of winter. Containers can be insulated in similar fashion for both situations. Some materials are better insulators than others. Rot-resistant wood such as cedar makes an attractive container that offers protection from excessive heating and cooling. Other containers may need help keeping the roots cool. One container placed into another with a minimum of 1" of space between the containers for insulating material such as moistened vermiculite, sawdust or Styrofoam packing peanuts is effective. The inside of a container may be lined with stiff foam insulation for straight-sided containers or lined with a couple of layers of carpet underlay for curved-sided containers. Coastal gardeners, because of the mild climate, can use a couple of overlapping layers of bubble wrap.

Protecting Containers from Frost Damage

Clay containers are subject to frost damage. Any water that has been absorbed by the container will expand as it freezes, causing cracks and chips. Avoid any containers with narrow openings. When moist soil in the container is subjected to freezing temperatures it will expand, which can crack even the most sturdy clay or stone container. An opening that is equal to or larger than the rest of the container will allow freezing soil to expand upward rather than out.

Protecting Tender Plants from Frost Damage

Protecting plants from frost is relatively simple. Cover them overnight with sheets, towels, burlap, row covers or even cardboard boxes. Refrain from using plastic because it doesn't retain heat and therefore won't provide your plants with any insulation. You can also move your containers to a frost-free area, such as a garage, garden shed or greenhouse.

Tender plants, including tropicals, may have to be moved indoors in winter. Tender evergreen plants can be lifted or dug from their respective containers, repotted and brought into the shelter of a greenhouse or the sunniest, warmest location in your house before the first frosts occur in fall. Most tender plants can be treated as houseplants, whether they return outdoors the following season or not. If you're without space to overwinter large, tender plants indoors, cuttings can be taken in late summer and grown as smaller plants for the following spring.

Some gardeners will grow their tender plants in partial shade outdoors so that the plants will be used to the lower light levels when brought inside for the winter season. This applies to plants that you wish to be ornamental inside your home as well as outside.

Preparing for Winter

Storing Containers

Containers that will be emptied at the end of the growing season can be cleaned and moved to a suitable storage spot. This will help prolong the life of the containers. Containers that

can't be moved and have no plants can be emptied of planting mix and cleaned. Ensure all containers are in good condition, and if needed, repairs can be done during the winter months. In areas that experience freezing temperatures, clay containers, especially decorative glazed containers, should be emptied of soil and stored indoors.

Overwintering Hardy Trees, Shrubs and Perennials

Hardy trees, shrubs and perennials that you intend to overwinter will survive winter better if the plants are allowed to harden as winter approaches. This means reducing the amount of water and fertilizer the plants receive through late summer and fall, which signals the plants to prepare themselves for the coming cold weather.

When the outside temperature drops below 32° F, planting mix can freeze solid. Plants continue to use water throughout winter, and even hardy plants can be killed, as frozen planting

This might not be the best storage for terra-cotta containers (left). Make sure the container is big enough to protect the plant's roots (right).

mix does not allow the plants to take up moisture. Containers that have a large enough volume of planting mix will increase the chances of the plants surviving winter. Water dry containers as soon as the planting mix thaws.

Overwintering Tender Rhizomes, Bulbs, Corms and Tubers

Perennials that grow from tender rhizomes, bulbs, corms or tubers can be dug up in fall after the top growth dies back, stored over winter and replanted in spring. If there is a chance that the container may freeze, dig up the tubers, bulbs, rhizomes, or corms. Shake the loose dirt from the roots and let them dry in a cool, dark place. Once dry, the rest of the soil should brush away. You can dust these modified underground stems with an antifungal powder, such as garden sulfur (found at garden centers), before storing them in moist peat moss or coarse sawdust. Keep them in a cool, dark, dry place that doesn't freeze. Check on them once a month, and lightly spray the storage medium with water if they appear very dry. If they start to sprout, pot them and keep them in moist soil in a bright window. They should be potted by late winter or early spring so that they will be ready for the outdoors. Some gardeners will leave the tubers, etc., in the containers and store the whole containers inside over winter.

Pests and Diseases

Green lacewings are beneficial predators.

Your container garden may experience attacks from pests and diseases. This need not be a traumatic event, as there are numerous ways of dealing with any problems that arise. You should not have to worry about soil-borne pests and diseases; they are almost non-existent in container gardens, especially when using soil-less planting mixes.

Annuals are planted each spring, and different species are often grown each year, so it can be difficult for pests and diseases to find their preferred host plants and establish a population. On the other hand, if you grow a lot of one particular annual species, any problems that do set in over summer may attack all the plants.

Perennials, trees and shrubs are both an asset and a liability when it comes to pests and diseases. Containers often contain a mixture of different plant species. Because many insects and diseases attack only one species of plant, mixed containers make it difficult for pests and diseases to find their preferred hosts and establish a population. But the plants are in the same container for a number of years, and any problems that do

Aphids.

Adult ladybird beetle.

develop can become permanent. Yet, if allowed, beneficial insects, birds and other pest-devouring organisms can also develop permanent populations.

Integrated Pest (or Plant) Management (IPM) is a moderate approach for dealing with pests and diseases. The goal of IPM is to reduce pest problems to levels of damage acceptable to you. Attempting to totally eradicate pests is a futile endeavor. Consider whether a pest's damage is localized or covers the entire plant. Will the damage kill the plant, or is it only affecting the outward appearance? Can the pest be controlled without chemicals?

IPM includes learning about your plants and the conditions they need for healthy growth. Some plant problems arise from poor maintenance practices. For example, overwatering saps plants of energy and can cause yellowing of the plant from the bottom up.

It is also useful for you to learn what pests might affect your plants, where and when to look for those pests and how to control them. Keep records of pest damage because your observations can reveal patterns useful in spotting recurring problems and in planning your maintenance regime.

Prevention and Control

The first line of defense for your plants is to prevent pests and diseases from attacking in the first place. The best way to accomplish this is to provide the conditions necessary for healthy plant growth. Healthy plants are able to fend well for themselves and can sustain some damage. Plants that are stressed or weakened are more subject to attack. Begin by choosing pest-resistant plants. Keep your soil healthy by using plenty of good-quality compost. Spray your plant's foliage with high-quality, fungally-dominated compost tea or fish emulsion. This acts as a foliar feed and also prevents fungal diseases.

Other cultural practices can help prevent pest attacks. Provide enough space for your plants so that they have good air circulation around them and are not stressed from competing for available resources. Remove plants that are decimated by pests and dispose of diseased foliage and branches. Keep your gardening tools clean and tidy up fallen leaves and dead plant matter in and around your permanently planted containers at the end of every growing season.

Powdery mildew.

Ladybird beetle larva.

Physical controls are generally used to combat insect and mammal problems. An example of such a control is picking insects off plants by hand, which is easy if you catch the problem when it is just beginning. Large, slow insects are particularly easy to pick off. You can squish or rub off colonies of insects with your fingers. Other physical controls include traps, barriers, scarecrows and natural repellants that make a plant taste or smell bad to pests. Garden centers offer a wide array of such devices. Physical control of diseases usually involves removing the infected plant or parts of the plant to keep the problem from spreading.

Biological controls make use of populations of natural predators. Birds, spiders and many insects help keep pest populations at a manageable level. Encourage these creatures to take up permanent residence in or near your garden, even though it may be difficult on balcony and rooftop gardens. Bird baths and feeders encourage birds to visit your container garden and feed on a wide variety of insect pests. Many

beneficial insects are already living in or near your garden, and you can encourage them to stay and multiply by planting appropriate food sources. Many beneficial insects eat nectar from flowers.

Chemical controls should be used only as a last resort. Pesticide products can be either organic or synthetic. If you have tried the other suggested methods and still wish to take further action, try to use organic types, which are available at most garden centers.

Chemical or organic pesticides may also kill the beneficial insects you have been trying to attract. Many people think that because a pesticide is organic, they can use however much they want. An organic spray kills because it contains a lethal toxin. NEVER overuse any pesticide. When using pesticides, follow the manufacturer's instructions carefully and apply in the recommended amounts only to the pests listed on the label. A large amount of pesticide is not any more effective in controlling pests than the recommended amount.

PROVEN WINNERS

PROVEN WINNERS

About this Guide

This book showcases 115 plants suitable for container gardening in Washington and Oregon. The plants are organized alphabetically by their most familiar common names. Scientific or botanical names appear in italics after the primary reference, and additional common names, if they exist, are listed with the features of each entry. This system enables those who are familiar with only the common name of a plant to find that plant easily in the book. However, readers are strongly encouraged to learn the botanical names. Common names are sometimes shared by several different plants, and they can change from region to region. Only the botanical name defines the specific plant everywhere on the planet.

The illustrated **Plants at a Glance** section at the beginning of the book allows you to quickly familiarize yourself with

the different plants, and it will help you find a plant if you're unsure of its name.

Clearly indicated within each entry are the plant's height and spread ranges, outstanding features and hardiness zone(s). At the back of the book, you will find a **Quick Reference Chart** that summarizes different features and requirements of the plants; you will find this chart handy when planning what is best for your container gardening designs.

Each entry gives clear instructions for planting and growing the plants in a container garden and recommends many of our favorite selections. Note: if height and spread ranges or hardiness zones are not given for each recommended plant, assume these values are the same as the ranges given with the features of each entry. If unsure, check with your local garden center experts when making your selections.

PROVEN WINNERS (OPPOSITE PAGE)

Plant Directory

African Daisy
Osteospermum

African daisies, with their unique colors, really stand out in a mixed container.

Growing
African daisy grows best in **full sun**. The potting mix should be **light, moist** and **well drained**. Fertilize every two weeks with half-strength fertilizer. Deadhead to encourage new growth and more flowers. Young plants can be pinched to encourage bushiness.

Tips
African daisies mix well with other annuals like petunia and verbena, or with other daisy-like flowers for a daisy-themed container. African daisy blooms best during cool weather and will brighten up your containers in early spring and in fall when other plants start to fade.

Recommended
O. ecklonis can grow upright to almost prostrate. The species is almost never grown in favor of its cultivars. **'Passion Mix'** includes heat-tolerant plants with pink, rose, purple or white flowers with deep blue centers and was an All-America Selections winner in 1999. **Starwhirls Series** has unique, spoon-shaped petals.

O. SOPRANO SERIES are robust, upright but compact plants that have regular or spoon-shaped petals in white and shades of purple.

O. **Symphony Series** has mound-forming, heat-tolerant plants that flower well throughout summer. **'Lemon'** bears yellow flowers. **'Orange'** bears tangerine orange flowers. **'Peach'** bears peachy pink flowers. **'Vanilla'** bears white flowers.

O. SOPRANO LIGHT PURPLE from the Proven Winners Selection SOPRANO SERIES

You may find African daisy listed as either Dimorphotheca *or* Osteospermum. Dimorphotheca *is a closely related genus that formerly included all the plants now listed as* Osteospermum.

Features: white, peach, orange, yellow, pink, lavender or purple flowers, often with darker centers **Height:** 12–20" **Spread:** 10–20" **Hardiness:** perennial or subshrub grown as an annual

Agapanthus
Agapanthus

A. campanulatus hybrid

Even when not in bloom, agapanthus contributes clumps of bright green foliage to mixed containers, providing a lush background for companions with lots of flowers but sparse foliage or for taller plants with leggy lower limbs.

Agapanthus is derived from the Greek words agape, *meaning "love," and* anthos, *meaning "flower."*

Growing

Agapanthus grows well in **full sun, partial shade** or **light shade**. Provide protection from the hottest afternoon sun. The potting mix should be **moist**

Also called: lily-of-the-Nile **Features:** clump-forming perennial; bright green, strap-like leaves; purple, blue or white, mid- to late-summer flowers **Height:** 12–36" **Spread:** 12–18" **Hardiness:** zones 7–10

A. *campanulatus* hybrid (above & below)

and **well drained**. Roots may rot in poorly drained containers. Fertilize weekly during the growing season with half-strength fertilizer.

Move containers to a sheltered location during frosty weather where plants are hardy. They can be lifted in fall and stored for re-planting in spring or stored in their containers in a cold but frost-free location in areas where they are not hardy.

Tips

Agapanthus makes an excellent filler plant. The strap-like leaves are bright green, and the rounded or pendulous clusters of flowers atop long, straight stems make excellent companions to flowering shrubs and large, shrub-like perennials.

Recommended

A. 'Blue Triumphator' forms a dense clump of foliage and bears loose clusters of bright blue flowers.

A. 'Bressingham White' forms a dense clump of foliage and bears loose clusters of white flowers.

A. campanulatus forms a dense clump of gray-green foliage and produces loose clusters of flowers in shades of blue, purple or sometimes white. 'Albovittatus' has white-margined leaves.

A. 'Lilliput' is a dwarf hybrid that grows 12–18" tall with an equal spread. It bears rounded clusters of deep blue flowers.

Angel's Trumpet

Brugmansia, Datura

All angel's trumpets add an exotic accent to the garden with their elegant, trumpet-shaped flowers.

Growing

Angel's trumpet grows best in **full sun**. The potting mix should be **moist** and **well drained**. Fertilize every two weeks with quarter- to half-strength fertilizer. Angel's trumpet is frost-tender, but *B. x candida* can be overwintered in a bright, cool room indoors.

Tips

Angel's trumpet flowers tend to open and be most fragrant at night. Place containers where you will enjoy them in the evening—near a patio, on a balcony or on a deck. They make excellent companions for other annuals.

Recommended

B. x candida (*B. aurea* x *B. versicolor*) is a large, woody plant that can grow up to 10' tall in a container and can be pruned to keep it smaller. It bears fragrant, white flowers that often open only on summer evenings. Many cultivars are available.

B. **'Charles Grimaldi'** is a woody plant with large, funnel-shaped, lemon yellow flowers. It grows up to 10' tall.

D. metel is an annual plant that easily self-seeds. It grows 3–4' tall and wide and produces white flowers in summer.

D. metel with petunias and impatiens

All parts of the plants, and especially the seeds, contain alkaloids that, if ingested, can cause liver damage, neurotoxicity and death. Avoid using these highly poisonous plants in places children frequent.

Also called: datura, trumpet flower
Features: bushy habit; white, yellow or purple, trumpet-shaped flowers   **Height:** 2–10'
Spread: 2–4'   **Hardiness:** tender annual; woody shrub grown as an annual

Arborvitae
Thuja

T. plicata SPRING GROVE, a Proven Winners Color Choice Selection

Arborvitae can usually only be grown in containers for three to five years, after which it will need to be planted in the ground, or it is likely to die.

Also called: cedar **Features:** evergreen shrub or small tree **Height:** 12"–10'
Spread: 12"–4' **Hardiness:** zones 3–8

These beautiful evergreens, with their soft foliage that won't poke you in close quarters, have dozens of dwarf cultivars that can last for several years in a big enough container.

Growing
Arborvitae grows well in **full sun, partial shade** or **light shade** in a sheltered location. The potting mix should be **moist** and **well drained**. Keep plants well watered. Fertilize with a weak fertilizer no

more than monthly in spring and early summer. Overwinter outdoors in a location out of strong winds and bright sun. Both can dry out the foliage and kill the plant. Protect plants from deer browsing, especially in early spring when these evergreens can be eaten to death.

Tips

Arborvitae is popular for use as a screening plant on decks and patios. It can be grown alone or combined with flowering perennials and annuals. The larger the container the better, because this woody plant consumes a lot of water.

Recommended

T. occidentalis (eastern white cedar) is a large, pyramidal tree with scale-like, evergreen needles. Many smaller and dwarf cultivars suitable for containers are available. **'Danica'** is a dwarf globe form growing to about 18" tall and wide with bright emerald green foliage. **'Emerald'** is narrow and upright and is considered one of the hardiest cultivars, more so if it doesn't dry out in winter. It grows about 10' tall and 36" wide before it needs transplanting to a garden. **'Teddy'** is a dwarf, rounded to oval plant, 12–18" tall and 24" wide, with fine, feathery, blue-green foliage that tinges bronze in winter.

T. plicata (western red cedar) has a few dwarf cultivars small enough for containers. The species and its cultivars are hardy only to zone 5. **'Cuprea'** is a low, mound-forming cultivar with bright yellow-tipped, bronzy green foliage. It grows about 36" tall and wide. **'Pygmaea'** has dark, blue-tinged foliage and grows 24–36" tall and 12–24" wide. **'Stoneham Gold'** grows about 6' tall and 36" wide. New growth emerges bright yellow and matures to dark green. **'Whipcord'** has long, pendulous, rope-like foliage that gives the plant a mop-like appearance. It grows about 36" tall and spreads about 30".

T. occidentalis cultivar (above)
T. occidentalis 'Danica' (below)

Argyranthemum
Argyranthemum

A. fructescens 'Butterfly' with million bells, sedum and others

The daisy-like flowers seem to suit almost any setting.

Growing

Argyranthemums prefer **full sun** but tolerate partial shade with decreased flowering. The potting mix should be **well drained**. Fertilize monthly with half-strength fertilizer. Pinch the plants back early on to encourage bushy growth.

Tips

Argyranthemums can be used as an accent to specimen plants or to add a colorful splash in mixed containers. They are lovely when massed in large container groupings or in window boxes on a sunny ledge.

Recommended

A. fructescens is a compact, rounded plant. It bears single, yellow-centered, daisy-like flowers with white petals. **'Butterfly,'** a Proven Winners Selection, produces canary yellow flowers. **'Gypsy Rose'** bears single, yellow-centered flowers with dark pink petals. **'Molimba Helio Double Pink'** bears light pink, double flowers that have a tufted appearance. **'Vanilla Butterfly'** bears single, yellow-centered, daisy-like flowers with creamy white petals that are pale yellow at the base.

Also called: marguerite daisy, cobbity daisy
Features: bushy habit; white, pink or yellow, summer flowers; divided to finely divided foliage **Height:** 16–36" **Spread:** 24–36"
Hardiness: subshrub grown as an annual

Cuttings can be taken in late summer and grown indoors over winter to be used the following summer.

Asparagus Fern
Asparagus

A. densiflorus 'Sprengeri' with begonias

Asparagus fern is actually not a fern but a member of the lily family and is closely related to edible asparagus.

Growing

Asparagus fern grows best in **light shade** or **partial shade** with protection from the afternoon sun. Avoid deep shade and direct sunlight. The potting mix should be kept evenly **moist** but allowed to dry out a little between waterings. Fertilize weekly during the growing season with quarter- to half-strength fertilizer. Overwinter indoors or throw away at the end of the season.

Tips

Vigorous growth makes asparagus fern a good filler plant for mixed containers; its unique appearance and habit add an interesting visual element to any combination.

Recommended

A. densiflorus is an arching, tender perennial with light green, feathery, leaf-like stems. Bright orange to red berries appear in fall. Two cultivars are commonly available. **'Myersii'** (foxtail fern) produces dense, foxtail-like stems that are 12–18" long. **'Sprengeri'** (emerald fern) has bright green, arching to drooping stems and a loose, open habit. It spreads 3–5' and is often grown where it will have room to hang.

Asparagus fern is a popular houseplant. It should be kept in bright but indirect light.

Features: fern-like habit; bright green, needle-like or narrow, leaf-like stems; inconspicuous flowers; inedible, bright orange to red berries **Height:** 12–36" **Spread:** 1–5' **Hardiness:** tender perennial grown as an annual

Bacopa
Sutera

S. cordata SNOWSTORM GIANT SNOWFLAKE with African daisy and fan flower

Bacopa grows under and around the stems of taller plants, forming a dense carpet dotted with tiny flowers, which eventually drifts over pot edges in a cascade of stars.

Growing
Bacopa grows best in **partial shade** with protection from the hot afternoon sun. The potting mix should be **moist** and **well drained**. Don't allow this plant to completely dry out; the leaves will die quickly if they become dry. Cutting back dead growth may encourage new shoots to form.

Tips
Bacopa is a popular plant for hanging baskets, mixed containers and window boxes. It forms an attractive, spreading mound.

Recommended
S. cordata forms a dense, compact mound of heart-shaped leaves with scalloped edges and bears tiny, white, star-shaped flowers along its neat, trailing stems. **'Cabana Trailing Blue'** bears blue or purple flowers. **'Lavender Showers'** bears pale lavender flowers. **'Olympic Gold'** has gold variegated foliage with white flowers. SNOWSTORM GIANT SNOWFLAKE, from Proven Winners, is a vigorous plant with large, white flowers. SNOWSTORM PINK has light pink flowers.

Features: white, lavender, purple, blue or pink flowers; decorative foliage; trailing habit
Height: 3–6"   **Spread:** 12–24"
Hardiness: tender perennial grown as an annual; can be overwintered near the coast if left in a protected location

Basil
Ocimum

The sweet, fragrant leaves of fresh basil add a delicious, licorice-like flavor to salads and tomato-based dishes.

Growing
Basil grows best in a warm, sheltered location in **full sun**. The potting mix should be **moist** and **well drained**. Fertilize weekly with half-strength fertilizer. Pinch tips and remove flower spikes regularly to encourage bushy growth.

Tips
Combine basil in a mixed container with other moisture-loving plants, or consider combining several different types of basil. Place a container of basil next to your potted tomatoes for an Italian-themed garden. Both plants produce the ingredients for bruschetta and other Italian dishes.

Recommended
O. basilicum is one of the most popular culinary herbs. There are dozens of varieties, including ones with large or tiny, green or purple, smooth or ruffled leaves, as well as varied flavors including anise, cinnamon and lemon. **'Green Globe'** forms a rounded mound of tiny leaves. **'Mammoth'** has huge leaves, up to 10" long and about half as wide. **'Purple Ruffles'** has dark purple leaves with frilly margins. **'Siam Queen'** is a cultivar of Thai basil with dark green foliage and dark purple flowers and stems.

O. basilicum 'Genovese' and *O. basilicum* 'Cinnamon'

Although basil will grow best in a warm spot outdoors, it can also be grown successfully in a bright window indoors to provide you with fresh leaves all year.

Features: bushy habit; fragrant, decorative leaves; pink, purple or white flowers
Height: 12–24"   **Spread:** 12–18"
Hardiness: tender annual

Bay Laurel
Laurus

L. nobilis

This shrub is an undemanding plant that is happily transferred from a sunny window indoors to a lightly shaded spot outdoors when the weather allows.

Growing

Bay laurel grows well in **light shade, partial shade** or **full sun** in a sheltered location. The potting mix should be **moist** and **well drained**. Fertilize monthly during the growing season with half-strength fertilizer. Plants will need to be overwintered indoors east of the Cascades, but may overwinter outdoors in a protected spot closer to the coast.

Tips

Bay laurel is an attractive, small shrub that is useful as a structural point in a mixed container and equally attractive when grown as a specimen. It can be pinched back to maintain a compact form or trained as a standard. Combine it with other herbs for a themed container or group of themed containers.

Recommended

L. nobilis is an aromatic, evergreen tree that can grow up to 40' tall where it is hardy. In a container, it stays much smaller and can be pruned to maintain a suitable size. **'Aurea'** has golden yellow foliage.

Bay leaves are familiar to most of us as the large, flat leaves we pick out of our stews or soups before serving.

Also called: sweet bay **Features:** tender, evergreen shrub; neat habit; undemanding **Height:** 12–36" **Spread:** 8–24" **Hardiness:** zones 8–10

Begonia

Begonia

B. x *tuberhybrida* cultivar with rubber plant, licorice plant, coleus, phormium and lamium

With beautiful flowers, a compact or trailing habit and decorative foliage, there is sure to be a begonia to fulfill your shade-gardening needs.

Growing

Begonias prefer **light to partial shade**, though wax begonias can be grown in full sun west of the Cascades. The potting mix should **neutral to acidic, humus rich** and **well drained**. Mix some compost into a peat-based potting mix. Fertilize every two weeks with quarter- to half-strength fertilizer.

The tubers of tuberous begonias can be uprooted when the foliage dies back and stored in slightly moistened peat moss over winter. The tuber will sprout new shoots in late winter and can be potted for another season. Rex begonias can be moved indoors and treated as house-plants in winter.

Tips

All begonias are useful for containers and planters on shaded patios, balconies,

---

Features: bushy habit; decorative foliage; red, pink, orange, yellow, apricot or white, sometimes bicolored (picotee) flowers
Height: 6–24" **Spread:** 6–24" **Hardiness:** tender perennial grown as an annual

B. hybrid (above), *B.* x *tuberhybrida* cultivar with phormium and others (below)

decks and porches. The trailing, tuberous varieties can be used in hanging baskets where the flowers can cascade over the edges.

Begonias thrive in the cool summer areas of western Washington and near the coast in Oregon better than anywhere else in the world, and they make great partners for shade-loving fuchsias. They do especially well in moss baskets.

Recommended

B. **Rex Cultorum hybrids** (rex begonias) are dense, mound-forming plants with dramatically patterned, high-contrast variegated foliage in shades of green, red, pink, white, bronze or purple. '**Escargot**' has spiraling, silver-striped, bronzy green leaves. '**Fire Flush**' has red-tinged, green and bronze variegated leaves. '**Fireworks**' has silvery white and purple-banded foliage.

B. x *semperflorens-cultorum* (wax begonias) are compact, mounded plants that have pink, white, red or bicolored flowers and green, bronze, reddish or white variegated foliage. They are more mildew and disease resistant than the tuberous begonias. They bloom continuously with no deadheading needed.

B. x *tuberhybrida* (tuberous begonias) form bushy mounds with green, bronze or purple foliage. The flowers can be held upright or in pendulous clusters. There are many hybrids of tuberous begonias available. **Non-stop Series** begonias are compact, bushy plants with red, yellow, apricot, orange, pink or white, double flowers. Two pendulous selections with flowers in a wide range of colors are '**Chanson,**' with single or semi-double flowers, and '**Illumination,**' with fully double flowers.

Bidens

Bidens

B. ferulifolia PETER'S GOLD CARPET

With fern-like foliage and pretty, golden flowers, this plant has a delicate appearance that belies its tough nature.

Growing

Bidens prefers **full sun** but will tolerate partial shade, bearing fewer flowers. The potting mix should be **moist** and **well drained**. Fertilize every two weeks with quarter- to half-strength fertilizer. If plants become lank and unruly in summer, shear them back lightly to encourage new growth and fall flowers.

Tips

Bidens is an absolute must for containers, window boxes and hanging baskets. Its fine foliage and attractive flowers make it useful for filling spaces between other plants.

Recommended

B. ferulifolia is a short-lived perennial that is used as an annual. Tufts of fern-like foliage are tipped with daisy-like, bright yellow flowers. **'Golden Goddess'** bears slightly larger flowers and narrower leaves. PETER'S GOLD CARPET, from Proven Winners, is a bushy, wide-spreading selection with deep golden yellow flowers. **'Solaire Compact Yellow'** is a low-growing plant with a mounding rather than trailing habit.

Bidens tolerates both cool, wet summers and extreme heat. It self-seeds easily and may pop up in your containers year after year, whether you want it to or not.

Features: bushy habit; feathery foliage; bright yellow flowers **Height:** 12–24"
Spread: 12–36" or more **Hardiness:** tender perennial grown as an annual

Black-Eyed Susan
Rudbeckia

R. hirta

As a cut flower, black-eyed Susan is long lasting in arrangements.

Features: summer through fall flowers in shades of yellow, orange, brown, red or gold, with brown or green centers **Height:** 12"–10' **Spread:** 12–36" **Hardiness:** zones 3–8; biennial or short-lived perennial treated as an annual

Bright and cheerful, black-eyed Susan provides a summer-long display of colorful flowers.

Growing

Black-eyed Susan grows well in **full sun** or **partial shade**. The potting mix should be **well drained**. Water regularly, though plants are fairly drought tolerant. Fertilize monthly with half-strength fertilizer. Pinch plants in June to encourage shorter, bushier growth.

Deadhead to keep the plants neat, to encourage more flower production and to minimize self-seeding.

Tips

Black-eyed Susan is a floriferous addition to mixed containers. It is good to use in containers with wildflower or native themes because it isn't unruly and won't become lank, floppy or messy, as some plants often do if grown in containers. The casual, country look of the blooms makes it a great plant to use in creative or recycled containers such as metal washtubs or old wheelbarrows.

Recommended

R. hirta (gloriosa daisy) forms a bushy mound of bristly foliage and bears bright yellow, daisy-like flowers with brown centers from summer through to the first hard frost in fall. **'Becky'** is a dwarf cultivar that grows up to 12" tall and has large flowers in solid and multi-colored shades of yellow, orange, red or brown. **'Cherokee Sunset'** was a 2002 All-America Selections winner. It bears semi-double and double flowers in all colors. **'Irish Eyes'** bears bright yellow flowers with green centers. This cultivar grows 24–30" tall and is best in larger containers where it will not look out of proportion. **Toto Series** are bushy, dwarf cultivars that grow 12–16" tall and bear single flowers with central brown cones and golden orange, lemon yellow or rich mahogany petals.

There are many more hybrids and species. *R. fulgida* var. *sullivantii* **'Goldsturm'** is a low maintenance, long-lived perennial that grows 24–30" tall and bears bright yellow, orange or red, brown-centered flowers. It is powdery mildew resistant. Other species grow 3–6' tall, making them less suitable for containers, but worth a try if you want to make a bold statement.

R. hirta with dahlia, sedum, fan flower and sedge (above), *R. hirta* 'Irish Eyes' (below)

Black-Eyed Susan Vine
Thunbergia

T. alata (far left)

Black-eyed Susan vine is a useful, flowering vine whose simple flowers dot the plant, giving it a cheerful, welcoming appearance.

Growing

Black-eyed Susan vine grows well in **full sun, partial shade** or **light shade**. For the most intense flower color, keep plants out of the hot afternoon sun. The potting mix should be **moist** and **well drained** and have some organic matter such as earthworm castings or compost mixed in. Fertilize every two weeks during the growing season with quarter-strength fertilizer. This plant can be overwintered indoors and then returned to the garden the following spring.

Tips

Black-eyed Susan vine can be trained to twine around railings and up trellises and small obelisks. It is attractive trailing down from mixed containers and hanging baskets.

Recommended

T. alata is a vigorous, twining climber. It bears yellow flowers, often with dark centers, in summer and fall. **'African Sunset'** has flower colors that range from deep brick red to warm pastel colors to cream. **'Alba'** bears white flowers with dark purple-brown centers. **Suzie Hybrids** bear large flowers in yellow, orange or white.

Features: twining, evergreen vine; attractive foliage; yellow, orange, white or sometimes red, summer to fall flowers   **Height:** 3–5'   **Spread:** 1–5'   **Hardiness:** tender perennial grown as an annual

Blood Grass
Imperata

Blood grass appears to glow red when backlit by the sun during the day or by a spotlight at night.

Growing

Blood grass grows best in **full sun** or **partial shade**. The potting mix should be kept **moist** but not wet. Mix in compost or earthworm castings because this grass likes organic matter in its soil. Fertilize every two weeks during the growing season with quarter-strength fertilizer. Pull out any growth that doesn't turn red because green growth is more vigorous and will tend to dominate. Cover containers or move them to a sheltered location in winter.

Tips

Blood grass mixes well in a grass-themed container and makes a good upright companion for bushy and trailing perennials and annuals. Its small size and non-invasive habit are welcome in mixed containers where more vigorous grasses can easily overwhelm other plants. Add it to pots of bamboo for an Asian-inspired container garden.

Recommended

I. cylindrica var. *rubra* (*I. cylindrica* 'Red Baron') forms slow-spreading clumps of slender leaves. The grass blades emerge bright green, tipped with red that spreads down the leaf as it matures, turning deep wine red by fall, then to copper in winter.

Blood grass is great for brightening up containers, adding color and texture offered by few other plants.

I. cylindrica var. *rubra* with sweet potato vine and spirea

Also called: Japanese blood grass
Features: perennial grass; colorful foliage; slender, upright habit   **Height:** 12–18"
Spread: 12"   **Hardiness:** zones 4–9

Blue Fescue
Festuca

F. glauca ELIJAH BLUE with Swan River daisy and nemesia

This fine-leaved, ornamental grass forms tufted clumps that resemble pincushions.

Growing

Blue fescue grows well in **full sun** or **partial shade**. The potting mix should be **moist** and **well drained**. Fertilize once a month during the growing season with half-strength fertilizer. This grass is fairly drought tolerant, if you are prone to forgetting to water quite as often as you should. Move fescue containers to a sheltered location out of the wind and sun in winter.

Features: tuft-forming, perennial grass; silvery or gray-blue to olive green or bright green foliage; spiky or relaxed habit
Height: 6–12"   **Spread:** 8–12"
Hardiness: zones 3–8

Tips

Blue fescue is an interesting accent plant for mixed containers. It adds unusual texture and color to annual and perennial combinations.

Recommended

F. filiformis (fine-leaf fescue) forms a low tuft of bright green, hair-like foliage. It grows 6–8" tall and spreads 8–12".

F. glauca (blue fescue) forms tidy, tufted clumps of fine, blue-toned foliage and produces short spikes of flowers in early summer. Cultivars and hybrids come in varying heights and in shades ranging from blue to olive green. ELIJAH BLUE, a Proven Selection by Proven Winners, and **'Boulder Blue'** have intense blue coloring. **'Skinner's Blue'** is one of the hardiest selections, making it a good choice for container culture.

Blue Oat Grass

Helictotrichon

H. sempervirens

Looking like a giant pincushion, blue oat grass has a strong architectural presence.

Growing

Blue oat grass thrives in **full sun**. The potting mix should be **well drained**. This grass thrives in poor soil and should be fertilized only once at the beginning of summer with half-strength fertilizer. Cover containers or move them to a sheltered location in winter.

Tips

The bushy, rounded form lends itself perfectly to being grown as a specimen in a large, urn-shaped container. It can also be combined with perennials and annuals as the centerpiece in a mixed container.

Recommended

H. sempervirens forms a large, dome-shaped clump of narrow, silvery blue leaf blades. Wiry, tan stems emerge from the center of the clump, bearing feathery, tan seedheads. **'Saphirsprudel'** ('Sapphire,' 'Sapphire Fountain') is sometimes described as being larger and more intensely blue than the species, while other growers claim they can see no difference between the species and the cultivar.

Blue oat grass is a tough, hardy grass and is one of the most likely to survive winter in a large container.

Features: perennial grass; cushion-like habit; brilliant blue foliage; decorative spikes of tan seedheads **Height:** 2–4' **Spread:** 24–30" **Hardiness:** zones 3–9

Bougainvillea
Bougainvillea

B. glabra

Place a strong obelisk in the center of the container to support this vine as it matures, allowing the other plants surrounding it to be seen.

Features: evergreen, attractive, sometimes variegated foliage; pink, white, yellow, apricot, red or purple flower bracts **Height:** 8"–8' **Spread:** 12–36" **Hardiness:** zones 9–11; tender vine grown as an annual or overwintered indoors

ach tiny bougainvillea flower is surrounded by three wavy, papery bracts. When it's in flower, the blooms can completely cover the plant.

Growing

Bougainvillea grows best in **full sun** but tolerates partial shade or light shade if it is kept indoors in winter. The potting mix should be **moist** and **well drained**. Mix in compost or earthworm castings. Fertilize every two weeks during the growing season with quarter- to half-strength fertilizer. This tender plant can be overwintered indoors or used as an annual.

Tips

Often purchased as a houseplant, this tender shrub really thrives when it is moved outdoors in summer. Bougainvillea is a lovely and adaptable plant as a specimen or when mixed with other plants. It can be trained as a trailing spreader, bushy shrub, standard or climbing vine.

Recommended

B. glabra is a tender, evergreen vine with semi-glossy leaves. The bracts may be white or magenta and are produced in mid- and late summer and sometimes again in winter. Where it is hardy, it can grow up to 26' tall. In containers, it isn't quite as vigorous and can be kept at a size you can accommodate. There are many hybrids available. **'Raspberry Ice'** has green leaves with irregular, creamy margins. The bracts are bright pink.

Bugleweed

Ajuga

A. reptans cultivar with a fern

Bugleweed's shade tolerance makes it particularly welcome in urban settings in places with limited sun exposure, such as on balconies and between buildings.

Growing

Bugleweed develops the best leaf color when grown in **partial shade** or **light shade** but tolerates full shade. Excessive sun may scorch the leaves. The potting mix should be **well drained**. Overwinter outdoors in a sheltered location.

Tips

Bugleweed will spread to fill in the spaces between plants in your mixed containers, and some selections will even trail over the edges of the container. The bold, colorful foliage can be used to create striking contrasts, such as pairing dark-leaved bugleweed with variegated or yellow-leaved hostas.

Recommended

A. pyramidalis 'Metallica Crispa' is slow-growing, with crinkly, bronze foliage and violet-blue flowers.

A. reptans is a low, quick-spreading plant with many colorful cultivars, such as **'Burgundy Glow,' 'Caitlin's Giant'** and **'Multicolor.'**

A. x tenorii is a hybrid with small leaves, a somewhat trailing habit and deep blue flowers. Available are the cultivars **'Chocolate Chip'** and **'Vanilla Chip.'**

Features: evergreen perennial; purple, pink, bronze, green, white, often variegated foliage; late-spring to early-summer flowers in purple, blue, pink or white **Height:** 3–12" **Spread:** 6–36" **Hardiness:** zones 3–8

Calla Lily
Zantedeschia

Z. *elliottiana* hybrid with pansies

Don't store all the rhizomes you lift in fall; these plants grow vigorously, and you may need only a few pieces for the following summer. The rest can be given to friends and family or composted.

Features: clump-forming habit; glossy, green foliage; summer flowers **Height:** 16–36" **Spread:** 8–24" **Hardiness:** tender, rhizomatous perennial grown as an annual

Calla lilies are exotic and elegant and lend a tropical touch to your container garden.

Growing
Calla lilies grow best in **full sun** in a sheltered location. The potting mix should be **moist** and **well drained** until the leaves have begun to unfurl. Once plants are actively growing, the soil can be kept quite wet. Fertilize every two

weeks with quarter- to half-strength fertilizer. Deadhead the faded flowers and stems.

Slowly reduce the water toward the end of summer to encourage dormancy and the foliage to die back. After a light frost, remove the foliage and stems from the rhizome, being careful not to damage it. Wash the rhizome gently under tepid water, removing soil and debris. Dust the rhizome with a fungicide and leave it to dry for a week at room temperature in a well-ventilated room. Once cured, store the rhizome in a paper bag in a cool, dark location at 41–50° F until it's time to plant it again in spring.

Tips

Calla lilies are stunning additions to large, colorful, mixed or specimen containers. For a theme garden, combine them with other water-loving plants such as elephant ears, rush and sweet flag to create a potted bog garden.

Recommended

Z. aethiopica forms a clump of glossy, green, arrow-shaped leaves. Ornamental, white spathes surround the creamy yellow flower spikes. Cultivars and hybrids are available.

Z. elliottiana (yellow calla, golden calla) forms a clump of white-spotted, dark green, heart-shaped leaves. Yellow spathes surround bright yellow flower spikes. This species is the parent plant of many popular hybrids.

Z. rehmannii (pink arum, pink calla) forms a clump of narrow, dark green leaves. White, pink or purple spathes surround yellow flower spikes. This species is also the parent of many hybrids.

Z. elliottiana hybrid with petunia, canna lily, dracaena and Swan River daisy (above)
Z. elliottiana hybrid (below)

Canna Lily
Canna

C. hybrid with lobelia

Canna lilies are stunning, dramatic plants that give an exotic flair to any garden.

Growing
Canna lilies grow best in **full sun**. The potting mix should be **moist** and **well drained**. Fertilize every two weeks with quarter- to half-strength fertilizer. Deadhead regularly to prolong blooming. Once all of the buds have opened and the flowers are finished, remove the stalk down to the next side shoot.

When planting, lay the rhizomes flat and just barely cover them with soil. Transplant canna lilies earlier than June to ensure they will flower before the end of the season.

Tips
Canna lilies can be included in large planters. They can be grown in containers of mixed canna lily varieties or used as focal points with bushy and trailing annuals.

Recommended
A wide range of canna lilies are available, including cultivars and hybrids with green, bronze, purple or yellow-and-green-striped foliage. Flowers may be white, red, orange, pink, yellow or sometimes bicolored. **Pfitzer Series** has dwarf selections that grow about 36" tall.

Features: green, blue-green, bronze, purple, yellow, sometimes variegated foliage; red, white, orange, pink, yellow or sometimes bicolored flowers **Height:** 3–7' **Spread:** 18–36" **Hardiness:** zones 7–11; tender, rhizomatous perennial grown as an annual

The silvery foliage of dusty miller and licorice plant creates an excellent backdrop for the colorful canna lily. Pairing coleus with canna lily gives a container a bold, tropical look.

Catch-Fly
Silene

The flowers of this plant are attractive to hummingbirds, butterflies and other pollinating insects.

Growing

Catch-fly grows well in **full sun** or **light shade**. The potting mix should be **moist** and **well drained**. Fertilize every two weeks with quarter- to half-strength fertilizer.

Tips

Catch-fly makes a good filler plant in mixed containers. This annual may turn up in your containers year after year because it tends to self-seed.

Recommended

S. armeria (sweet William catch-fly) forms a basal rosette of gray-green leaves from which many sticky stems emerge. It bears clusters of vivid pink flowers. **'Electra'** bears more flower clusters than the species.

S. coeli-rosa (rose-of-heaven) is an upright plant with slender, gray-green foliage. Flowers are bright pink with paler, often white centers. **'Blue Angel'** bears blue flowers. **'Rose Angel'** bears bright pink flowers.

S. pendula (nodding catch-fly) is a low-growing, bushy, mounding or spreading plant. It bears loose clusters of nodding, single or double, light pink flowers. **'Peach Blossom'** has flowers that open a deep pink and gradually fade to white as they mature, with flowers in different stages of coloration showing at once. **'Snowball'** bears double, white flowers.

S. pendula 'Peach Blossom'

Catch-fly helps keep pest populations down by attracting beneficial insects and even by catching small insects on its sticky stems and leaves, which makes it a favorite with children.

Features: bushy, spreading or upright habit; loose or dense clusters of deep to light pink or white flowers   **Height:** 6–24"
Spread: 6–18"   **Hardiness:** annual

Cilantro • Coriander
Coriandrum

The delicate, cloud-like clusters of flowers attract pollinating insects such as butterflies and bees as well as abundant predatory insects that will help keep pest insects at a minimum in your garden.

Growing

This herb prefers **full sun** but tolerates partial shade. The potting mix should be **light** and **well drained**. Fertilize monthly with half-strength fertilizer. This plant dislikes humid conditions and does best during a dry summer.

Tips

This species has pungent leaves and is best planted where people will not have to brush past it. It is, however, a delight to behold when in flower and is an excellent plant for adding volume to your mixed planters. The airy clouds of white flowers create a lovely backdrop for bright red, pink or purple flowers.

Recommended

C. sativum forms a clump of lacy basal foliage above which large, loose clusters of tiny, white flowers are produced. The seeds ripen in late summer and fall.

C. sativum

C. sativum is a popular culinary herb. The leaves, called cilantro, are used in salads, salsas and soups, and the seeds, called coriander, are used in pies, chutneys and marmalades. The flavor of each is quite distinct.

Features: form; foliage; flowers; seeds
Height: 16–24"   **Spread:** 8–16"
Hardiness: tender annual

Clematis
Clematis

C. integrifolia

Climbing vines can be truly stunning growing up an obelisk or other trellis from a container, and though gardeners have reported mixed results treating clematis this way, the possibility of success makes it worth a try.

Growing
Clematis prefers **full sun** but tolerates full shade. Try to keep the container in the shade because this plant does best when its roots stay cool. The potting mix should be **moist** and **well drained**

and have some organic matter like compost mixed in. Fertilize every two weeks during the growing season with quarter- to half-strength fertilizer.

This hardy plant has sensitive roots. Freezing and thawing will more likely

---

Features: twining vine or bushy perennial; attractive, leafy habit; flowers in shades of blue, purple, pink, white, yellow or red or sometimes bicolored **Height:** 1–5' **Spread:** 1–4' **Hardiness:** zones 3–8

C. x jackmanii (above), *C. integrifolia* (below)

kill your clematis vine than extreme cold. Move the container to a location where the temperature will stay fairly even, such as a protected patio or porch near the coast or an unheated garage or shed east or west of the Cascades.

Tips
Clematis makes a lovely addition to a mixed container, where you can grow it up an obelisk or trellis or let it spill over the edge. The abundant flowers make this plant worth including in your containers even if it survives only a few years.

Recommended
C. alpina (alpine clematis) is a twining vine that blooms in spring and early summer, bearing bell-shaped, blue flowers with white centers.

C. integrifolia (solitary clematis) is a bushy perennial, rather than a climbing vine, though it has flexible, trailing growth that can be trained to grow up a low trellis or spill over the edge of a container. It bears flared, bell-shaped, purple flowers in summer.

C. x *jackmanii* (Jackman clematis) is a twining vine that bears large, purple flowers in summer. Many hybrids are available, with flowers in a wide range of colors.

C. viticella **Raymond Evison Patio Clematis™ Collection** are slow-growing, twining, compact vines that grow 3–4' tall and 18–36" wide and are hardy to zone 4. The cultivars **'Angelique,' 'Parisienne,' 'Chantilly,' 'Cezanne,' 'Picardy,' 'Versailles'** and **'Bourbon'** bloom well into fall in varied shades of magenta, purple and purple-blue.

Combine two clematis selections together to provide a mix of tone and texture.

Cleome
Cleome

reate a bold, exotic display in your garden with these lovely and unusual flowers.

Growing
Cleome prefers **full sun** but tolerates partial shade. The potting mix should be **moist** and **well drained**. These plants are drought tolerant but look and perform best if watered regularly. Fertilize monthly with quarter-strength fertilizer. Pinch out the center of the plant when transplanting, and it will branch out to produce up to a dozen blooms. Deadhead to prolong the blooming period.

Tips
Cleome is an interesting plant to use as the central or focal plant in a mixed container.

Recommended
C. hassleriana is a tall, upright plant with strong, supple, thorny stems. The foliage and flowers of this plant have a strong, but pleasant, scent. Flowers are borne in loose, rounded clusters at the ends of leafy stems. Many cultivars are available. **'Helen Campbell'** has white flowers. **Royal Queen Series** bear fade-resistant flowers in all colors. **'Sparkler Blush'** is a dwarf cultivar that grows up to 36" tall. It bears pink flowers that fade to white.

C. serrulata (Rocky Mountain bee plant) is native to western North America. It is rarely available commercially. The thornless dwarf cultivar **'Solo'** is available to be grown from seed. It grows 12–18" tall and bears pink and white blooms.

C. hassleriana with nicotiana, geranium and impatiens

"Hummingbird flower" might be a more appropriate name for this plant. It blooms through fall, providing nectar for the tiny birds after many other flowers have finished blooming.

Also called: spider flower   **Features:** bushy, upright habit; scented, divided foliage; pink, rose, violet or white flower clusters **Height:** 1–5'   **Spread:** 18–36" **Hardiness:** annual

Clover
Trifolium

T. repens 'Dark Dancer' with coleus and others

Growing

Clover is best grown in **full sun to partial shade**. The potting mix should be **moist, well drained** and **neutral**. Fertilize once during the growing season, about a month after you plant it out, with half-strength fertilizer. Move it to a sheltered location in winter, or throw it away after the first frost and plant new clover the following summer.

Tips

This lovely little plant will add interest to mixed containers. It is especially striking when grouped with other plants with dramatically colored foliage or bright, contrasting flowers.

Recommended

T. repens is a low, spreading perennial often grown as an annual. It is rarely grown in favor of the many attractive cultivars. The small, rounded flower clusters can be pink, red, yellow or white. **'Dark Dancer'** ('Atropurpureum') has a dwarf habit and dark burgundy leaves with lime green margins. **'Salsa Dancer'** produces bright green foliage with burgundy and white markings in the center of each leaf and bears white flowers.

Because of its small stature, clover can be lost to the eye when mixed with other plants in beds but seems to stand out when planted in containers, both as a specimen and when mixed with other annuals.

Features: spreading habit; decorative, often variegated foliage; small, globe-shaped, white, pink, red or yellow flowers   **Height:** 3–12"   **Spread:** 12–18" or more   **Hardiness:** zones 4–8; perennial grown as an annual

Because of its invasive nature, clover is ideally suited to container culture. You can control the roots of clover and other ornamental groundcovers in containers by inserting chipped saucers or small plates into the soil to serve as an underground root barrier. Let the top half of the crockery poke above the soil as a charming accent in the pot.

Coleus
Solenostemon (Coleus)

Coleus has always been available in a great range of colors, and it is only more desirable as new varieties emerge onto the market in colors such as plum, burgundy, chartreuse, gold, lime, copper, wine and almost black.

Growing

Coleus prefers to grow in **light shade** or **partial shade** but tolerates full shade if not too dense and full sun if the plants are watered regularly. The foliage color will be deeper and more intense when grown in the shade. The potting mix should be **humus rich, moist** and **well drained**. Mix in some compost or earthworm castings.

These plants are perennials that are grown as annuals, but they also make attractive houseplants. Cuttings taken from favorites in late summer can be grown indoors in a bright room by a sunny window.

Tips

The bold, colorful foliage creates a dramatic display when several different selections are grouped together in a single container or group of containers. Coleus also makes an excellent accent plant in a mixed container with other annuals or perennials.

When flower buds develop, it is best to pinch them off because the plants tend to stretch out and become less attractive after they flower.

S. scutellarioides SEDONA

Coleus can be trained into a tree form. Pinch off the lower leaves and side branches as they grow to create a long, bare stem with leaves on only the upper half. Once the plant reaches the desired height, pinch from the top to create a bushy, rounded crown.

Features: bushy habit; colorful, often variegated foliage in shades of green, yellow, pink, red, burgundy or purple   **Height:** 6–36"   **Spread:** 6–24"   **Hardiness:** tender perennial grown as an annual

Recommended

S. scutellarioides (*Coleus blumei* var. *verschaffeltii*) cultivars and hybrids form bushy mounds of foliage. The leaf edges range from slightly toothed to very ruffled. The leaves are usually multi-colored with shades ranging from pale greenish yellow to deep purple-black. Plants grow 6–36" tall, depending on the cultivar, and the spread is usually equal to the height. Some interesting cultivars include **'Black Prince,'** with deep purple, almost black foliage; **'Fishnet Stockings,'** with purple-veined, bright green foliage; **'Merlin's Magic,'** with deeply divided, slightly ruffled, purple, pink, burgundy or yellow and green variegated foliage; and SEDONA, a Proven Selection by Proven Winners, with pink-veined, orange foliage.

S. scutellarioides cultivar with begonia and fig (above)
S. scutellarioides cultivar with coral bells and others (below)

Coral Bells
Heuchera

H. AMBER WAVES, from Proven Winners, alone and with African daisy, in front of sedge (above), *H.* hybrid with sweet potato vine, begonia and sweet flag (below)

From soft yellow-greens and oranges to midnight purples and silvery, dappled maroons, coral bells offer a great variety of foliage options.

Growing

Coral bells grow best in **light shade** or **partial shade**. Foliage colors can bleach out in full sun. The potting mix should be **neutral to alkaline, moist** and **well drained**. Mix in some compost or earthworm castings. Fertilize once a month during the growing season with quarter- to half-strength fertilizer. Cover or move to a sheltered location in winter.

Also called: heuchera, alum root
Features: mound-forming or spreading perennial; scalloped or heart-shaped, colorful foliage; red, pink, purple, white or yellow, small, summer flowers   **Height:** 1–4'
Spread: 12–18"   **Hardiness:** zones 3–8

Tips

Coral bells make attractive additions to mixed containers. The colorful foliage contrasts particularly well with grasses, ferns and yellow-flowered plants like lady's mantle, iris and dahlia. Combine different selections of coral bells for an interesting display. The persistent foliage of coral bells is excellent for providing much-needed color for winter container gardens.

Recommended

There are many hybrids and cultivars of coral bells available. The following are just a few of the possibilities. **'Caramel'** has apricot-colored foliage and pink flowers. **'Chocolate Ruffles'** has ruffled, glossy brown foliage with purple undersides that give the leaves a bronzed appearance. **'Coral Cloud'** forms a clump of glossy, crinkled leaves and bears pinkish red flowers. **'Firefly'** develops a clump of dark green leaves with attractive, fragrant, bright pinkish red flowers. Both **'Lime Rickey'** and DOLCE KEY LIME PIE, from Proven Winners, form a low mass of chartreuse leaves. **'Marmalade'** has foliage that emerges red and matures to orange-yellow. **'Montrose Ruby'** has bronzy purple foliage with bright red undersides. **'Northern Fire'** has red flowers and leaves mottled with silver. **'Obsidian'** has lustrous, dark purple, nearly black foliage. **'Pewter Veil'** has silvery purple leaves with dark gray veins. Its flowers are white flushed with pink. **'Velvet Night'** has dark purple leaves with a metallic sheen and creamy white flowers.

Coral bells are delicate-looking woodland plants and can be combined with other woodland plants such as ferns to create a themed container.

H. DOLCE KEY LIME PIE **with sedge and African daisy**

Crocosmia

Crocosmia

The intense colors of crocosmia are a beacon in the garden and create a brilliant display in a container.

Growing

Crocosmias prefer **full sun** in a sheltered location. The potting mix should be **humus rich, moist** and **well drained**. Fertilize monthly during the growing season with half-strength fertilizer. Move plants to a sheltered location in winter. These plants will be short-lived in containers.

Tips

These attractive, unusual plants create a striking display when planted by themselves in large containers or in mixed containers with other perennials.

Recommended

C. x crocosmiflora is a spreading plant with long, strap-like leaves. It grows 18–36" tall, and the clump spreads about 12". One-sided spikes of red, orange or yellow flowers are borne in mid- and late summer. **'Citronella'** ('Golden Fleece') bears bright yellow flowers.

C. **'Lucifer'** is the hardiest of the bunch and bears bright scarlet flowers. It grows 3–4' tall, with a spread of about 18".

If you've had no luck overwintering crocosmia, the problem may be that the corms get too wet. Drag the pot to a dry spot such as under the eaves or beneath a patio table for winter. Also, the corms can be dug up in fall and stored in slightly damp peat moss in a cool, dark place during winter.

C. 'Lucifer'

Features: cormous, semi-tender perennial; red, orange or yellow flowers in mid- to late summer; bright green, strap-like leaves
Height: 18"–4'   **Spread:** 12–18"
Hardiness: zones 5–9

Cuphea
Cuphea

C. FLAMENCO RUMBA

his wonderful plant will attract hummingbirds and butterflies to your garden.

The genus name, Cuphea, *arises from the Greek word* kyphos, *meaning "curved." The name refers to the curved seed capsules.*

Features: tropical shrub; red, pink, purple, violet, green or white flowers   **Height:** 6–24"
Spread: 10–36"   **Hardiness:** tender shrub grown as an annual

Growing

Cuphea grows well in **full sun** or **partial shade**. The potting mix should be **moist** and **well drained**. Short periods of drought are tolerated. Fertilize monthly during the growing season with half-strength fertilizer. This plant is tender and can be treated like an annual or brought indoors at the end of summer and treated like a houseplant.

Tips

This is a good plant for container gardens with a tropical theme because it grows well with canna lily, banana and other plants with hot, bright colors.

Recommended

C. **hybrids** offer a differing selection from the species and cultivars in subtle ways, including flower color and habit. The FLAMENCO SERIES are Proven Selections from Proven Winners. FLAMENCO TANGO has bright purple-pink flowers. FLAMENCO RUMBA bears fiery red flowers with dark purple centers.

C. hyssopifolia (Mexican heather, false heather, elfin herb) is a bushy, branching plant that forms a flat-topped mound. The flowers have green calyces and light purple, pink or sometimes white petals. The plants bloom from summer to frost. **'Allyson Purple'** ('Allyson') is a dwarf plant that bears lavender flowers. **'Desert Snow'** has white flowers.

C. ignea (*C. platycentra*; cigar flower, firecracker plant) is a spreading, freely branching plant. Thin, tubular, bright red flowers are produced from late spring to frost. It can also be used as a houseplant.

Dahlia

Dahlia

D. hybrid with zinnia, nasturtium and thyme

The variation in size, shape and color of dahlia flowers is astonishing. With an estimated 58,000 selections, you are sure to find at least one or two that you just have to have for your containers.

Growing

Dahlias prefer **full sun**. The potting mix should be **humus rich, moist** and **well drained**. Fertilize every two weeks during the growing season with quarter-strength fertilizer. Deadhead to keep plants neat and to encourage more blooms.

Dahlias are tender, tuberous perennials that are treated as annuals. The tubers

Dahlia cultivars span a vast array of colors, sizes and flower forms, but breeders have yet to develop true blue, scented and frost-hardy varieties.

Features: bushy habit; attractive foliage; summer flowers in shades of red, yellow, orange, pink, purple, white or sometimes bicolored **Height:** 8"–5' **Spread:** 8–24" **Hardiness:** tender, tuberous perennial grown as an annual

can be lifted in fall and stored over winter in slightly moist peat moss. Pot them and keep them in a bright room when they start sprouting in mid- to late winter. West of the Cascades, you can overwinter dahlias outdoors in pots just by storing them in a dry spot.

Tips
The sturdy, bushy growth of dahlias gives them a shrubby appearance that can be used to visually anchor a mixed container that includes softer-looking or trailing plants. The stunning flowers draw the eye and create a strong focal point, so use them in places you want people to see or notice. When using the taller dahlias in a large pot, you can support the heavy blooms with a wire tomato cage, or surround the plants with the some stiff upright plants such as *Sedum* 'Autumn Joy.'

Recommended
D. **hybrids** are bushy, tuberous perennials with glossy leaves in shades of green, bronze or purple. They are generally described by their flower shape, such as collarette, decorative or peony-flowered. The flowers are 2–12" and are available in shades of purple, pink, white, yellow, orange, red or bicolored. **'Amazon Pink and Rose'** is a miniature plant with yellow-centered, pink, semi-double flowers. The petals are light pink with deep pink bases. **'Bishop of Llandaff'** has dark red, semi-double flowers and bronze foliage. **'Dalstar Yellow'** is a miniature plant with pale yellow, semi-double flowers. **'Dalina Mini Bahamas'** is a dwarf plant with glossy, green foliage and fuchsia pink, double flowers. **'David Howard'** has multi-tonal orange, double flowers that contrast strikingly with its dark purple foliage. **'Figaro'** can be started from seed and has double and semi-double flowers in a wide range of colors.

D. 'Chic' (above), *D.* hybrids with lobelia and dracaena (below)

Daylily

Hemerocallis

he daylily's adaptability and durability, combined with its variety in color, blooming period, size and texture, explain its popularity.

Growing

Daylilies grow in any light from **full sun to full shade.** The deeper the shade, the fewer flowers will be produced. The potting mix should be **moist** and **well drained**, but these plants will tolerate both wet and dry conditions. Fertilize monthly during the growing season with half-strength fertilizer. Deadhead to encourage more flowering. Move containers to a sheltered location in winter.

Tips

Plant daylilies alone, or group them in containers. Although the small selections seem best suited to container culture, the larger plants make a bold statement and will grow equally well in containers.

Recommended

Daylilies come in an almost infinite number of sizes and colors over the range of species, cultivars and hybrids. They all form clumps of strap-like foliage and produce a cluster of buds on a stem that is held above the foliage. The buds open one at a time, and each lasts for a single day. **'Stella D'oro'** is a dwarf ever-blooming daylily perfect for pots.

H. fulva 'Flore Pleno'

More than 12,000 daylily selections have been developed, with sometimes hundreds more added yearly.

Features: clump-forming perennial; spring and summer flowers in every color except blue and pure white; grass-like foliage
Height: 1–4'   **Spread:** 1–4'
Hardiness: zones 2–9

Dogwood
Cornus

C. sericea 'Isanti'

Move dogwoods to an unheated garage or shed in winter, especially in the areas where the ground freezes, such as east of the Cascades and in cold mountain climates.

Features: deciduous large shrub or small tree; attractive, late-spring to early-summer flowers; fall foliage; stem color; fruit
Height: 3–10' in containers   **Spread:** 2–8' in containers   **Hardiness:** zones 2–8

Flowers, stem color, leaf variegation, fall color, growth habit, adaptability and hardiness are all positive attributes to be found in dogwoods.

Growing
Dogwoods grow well in **full sun, light shade** or **partial shade**, with a slight preference for light shade. The potting mix should be **humus rich, neutral to slightly acidic** and **well drained**. Mix

in compost or earthworm castings and fertilize monthly during the growing season with quarter-strength fertilizer. Move containers to a sheltered location in winter.

Tips

If you have very large containers or planters and want to grow a shrub or small tree, dogwoods are a good choice, though they may need a bit more pruning and training than they would in a garden. The larger dogwoods will probably outgrow a container and need to be moved to a garden in about three to five years, unless you root prune them every two or so years.

Recommended

C. alba (red-twig dogwood, Tartarian dogwood) and *C. sericea* (*C. stolonifera*; red-osier dogwood) species and cultivars are grown for their bright red stems that provide winter interest. Cultivars are available with stems in varied shades of red, orange or yellow. Fall foliage color can also be attractive.

C. alba 'Bud's Yellow' (above), *C. alba* 'Bailhalo' (below)

C. alternifolia (pagoda dogwood) can be grown as a large, multi-stemmed shrub or a small, single-stemmed tree. The branches have an attractive, layered appearance. Clusters of small, white flowers appear in early summer. The cultivar **'Argentia'** has silver and green variegated leaves. (Zones 3–8)

C. kousa (Kousa dogwood) is grown for its decorative flowers, fruit, fall color and interesting bark. The white-bracted flowers are followed by bright red fruit. The foliage turns red and purple in fall. **'Satomi'** has soft pink flowers. (Zones 5–8)

Dusty Miller
Senecio

S. *cineraria* 'Silver Dust'

Dusty miller makes an artful addition to container gardens. The soft, silvery gray, deeply lobed foliage creates a good backdrop to show off the brightly colored flowers or foliage of other plants.

Growing

Dusty miller prefers **full sun** but tolerates light shade. The potting mix should be **well drained**. Fertilize no more than once a month during the growing season with quarter-strength fertilizer. Pinch off the flowers before they bloom; the flowers aren't showy and steal energy that would otherwise go to the foliage.

Dusty Miller will overwinter in mild winter areas near the coast. Don't prune it until March, and then cut back the winter-weary foliage almost to the ground. By June, the plants will look fresh with new growth.

Tips

The soft, silvery, lacy leaves of dusty miller are its main feature, and it is used primarily as a contrast or backdrop plant.

Recommended

S. cineraria forms a mound of fuzzy, silvery gray, lobed or finely divided foliage. Many cultivars have been developed. **'Cirrus'** has lobed, silvery green or white foliage. **'Silver Dust'** has deeply lobed, silvery white foliage. **'Silver Lace'** has delicate, silvery white foliage that glows in the moonlight.

Features: bushy habit; variably lobed foliage in shades of silvery gray **Height:** 12–24"
Spread: equal to height or slightly narrower
Hardiness: tender annual

Dwarf Morning Glory

Convolvulus

If you love morning glory but don't want a climber, try this little cutie in containers and window boxes.

Growing

Dwarf morning glory prefers **full sun**. The potting mix must be **well drained**. Fertilize no more than once, about a month after planting, with quarter-strength fertilizer. This plant will produce lots of foliage but few flowers in soil that is too fertile.

Tips

Dwarf morning glory is a compact, mounding plant that can be grown in containers and hanging baskets. It makes a nice plant to grow alone in a small container and also mixes well with other annuals. The mounding to slightly trailing form looks good when combined with grasses.

Recommended

C. tricolor is a compact, mound-forming plant that bears trumpet-shaped flowers that last only a single day, opening in the morning and twisting shut that evening. **Ensign Series** has low-growing, spreading plants that grow about 6" tall. **'Royal Ensign'** has deep blue flowers with white and yellow throats. **'Star of Yalta'** bears deep purple flowers that pale to violet in the throat.

Although this plant is related to the noxious weed C. arvensis (bindweed), dwarf morning glory is not invasive or problematic.

C. tricolor

Features: mound-forming habit; blue, purple or pink, summer flowers sometimes variegated with yellow and white throats
Height: 6–16" **Spread:** 10–12"
Hardiness: annual

Elder
Sambucus

S. *nigra* BLACK BEAUTY with African daisy, coral bells
and euphorbia (above), S. *nigra* BLACK LACE (below)

Features: large, bushy, deciduous shrub;
early-summer flowers; edible fruit; colorful,
decorative foliage   **Height:** 2–10' in containers
Spread: 2–10' in containers   **Hardiness:**
zones 3–8

Elder is a versatile shrub that can be
trained to function as a small tree
in a container garden.

Growing
Elders grow well in **full sun** or **partial
shade**. Yellow-leaved cultivars and varieties develop the best color in light
shade or partial shade, and black-,
burgundy- or purple-leaved cultivars
develop the best color in full sun. The
potting mix should be **moist** and **well
drained**. Fertilize monthly during summer with quarter-strength fertilizer.
Stop fertilizing before fall to give the
plant time to harden off for winter.

Move containers to a sheltered location
for winter or cover them to protect them

from wind and temperature fluctuations. Prune plants back in spring to keep them at a suitable size. You may have to root prune them every few years or move them to a garden when they become too large for the container.

Tips

Elders make a strong architectural statement and are best suited to large containers. Train them as small, single- or multi-stemmed trees. Plant annuals with contrasting flower colors around the base of an elder for an eye-catching combination.

Recommended

S. canadensis (American elder), **S. nigra** (black elder) and **S. racemosa** (European red elder) are rounded shrubs with white or pink flowers followed by red or dark purple berries. Cultivars are available with green, yellow, bronze or purple foliage and deeply divided or feathery foliage. *S. canadensis* **'Lanciniata'** has lacy, green foliage that gives this shrub a fern-like or feathery appearance. **S. nigra** BLACK BEAUTY, a Proven Winners Color Choice Selection, has dark purple, almost black, foliage that darkens as summer progresses. *S. nigra* BLACK LACE, another Proven Winners Color Choice Selection, produces finely cut black foliage and pink flowers. **S. nigra 'Madonna'** bears dark green foliage with wide, irregular, yellow margins. **S. racemosa 'Sutherland Gold'** has deeply divided, yellow-green foliage.

Elderberries will attract birds to your garden.

S. *nigra* 'Madonna' (above)
S. *racemosa* 'Goldilocks' (center)

S. *nigra* BLACK BEAUTY (below)

Elephant Ears

Colocasia

This striking plant will add a tropical look to your patio, deck or balcony.

Growing

Elephant ears grow well in **light shade** or **full shade**. The potting mix should be **humus rich, slightly acidic** and **moist to wet**. Fertilize every two weeks during the growing season with quarter-strength fertilizer. Move elephant ears indoors in winter, or store the tuberous roots in a cool, dry location until spring.

Tips

Planted alone in a moist container or combined with other moisture-lovers, this plant makes a striking addition to any container garden.

Recommended

C. ecsulenta is a tuberous, warm-climate plant that produces a clump of large, heart-shaped leaves. Cultivars with red- or purple-veined to dark purple or bronze foliage are available. **'Black Magic'** has dark purple leaves. **'Fontanesii'** has green leaves with red to purple stems, veins and margins.

C. esculenta 'Illustris,' a Proven Winners Selection (above), *C. esculenta* with coleus, sweet potato vine and others (right)

Elephant ears are often included in water gardens and can be grown in up to 8" of water. Try them in a large water barrel if you want something other than miniature water lilies.

Also called: taro   **Features:** large, dark green to purple leaves   **Height:** 2–4'
Spread: 2–4'   **Hardiness:** tender, tuberous perennial grown as an annual

Euonymus
Euonymus

E. fortunei GOLD SPLASH

This group of variable shrubs includes some of the best-suited woody plants for container culture.

Growing

Euonymus prefers **full sun** but tolerates light shade or partial shade. The potting mix should be **moist** and **well drained**. Fertilize monthly during the growing season with quarter-strength fertilizer. Move this plant to a sheltered location out of the wind and sun in winter.

Tips

Burning bush has a neat, rounded habit and works well as the center plant in a large mixed container. Wintercreeper euonymus can be allowed to trail over the edge of a container or be trained to

Features: deciduous or evergreen shrub, small tree, groundcover or climber; decorative foliage; good fall color **Height:** 1–10' in containers **Spread:** 1–10' in containers **Hardiness:** zones 3–9

E. alatus FIRE BALL (above)
E. fortunei 'Emerald 'n' Gold' (center)

E. alatus (below)

climb a small trellis. It can also be pruned to form a small shrub or be trained as a topiary plant.

Wintercreeper euonymus is good for winter container gardens and can be planted in the same pots as spring-blooming bulbs. Its low-growing or creeping varieties are especially easy to root as cuttings. Just snip off an 8" section, remove the lowest leaves from the bottom third of the stem and poke the cutting into potting soil.

Recommended

E. alatus (burning bush, winged euonymus) is an attractive, open, mounding, deciduous shrub. It grows far too large to be suitable for a container, but there are several dwarf selections that can be used. **'Compacta'** ('Compactus') is a popular dwarf cultivar. It has dense, compact growth, reaching up to 10' tall and wide, though smaller with pruning and when grown in a container. FIRE BALL ('Select'), a Proven Winners Color Choice Selection, is a hardier selection of 'Compacta' that grows up to 7' tall and wide. It has brilliant red fall color. (Zones 3–8)

E. fortunei (wintercreeper euonymus) as a species is rarely grown in favor of the wide and attractive variety of cultivars. These can be prostrate, climbing or mounding evergreens, often with attractive, variegated foliage. BLONDY ('Interbolwji') has yellow foliage with narrow, irregular, dark green margins. **'Emerald Gaiety'** is a vigorous shrub that sends out long shoots that will attempt to scale any nearby surface. The foliage is bright green with irregular, creamy margins that turn pink in winter. **'Emerald 'n' Gold'** is a bushy selection that has green leaves with wide, gold margins. The foliage turns pinky red during winter and spring. (Zones 5–9)

Euphorbia

Euphorbia

Euphorbia has bright yellow flowers that emerge early in the season. In fall, its foliage turns bright shades of orange, red or purple.

Growing

Euphorbia grows well in **full sun** or **light shade**. The potting mix should be **humus rich, moist** and **well drained**. This plant is drought tolerant and rarely needs fertilizing. Fertilize once in the growing season, preferably just after

If you are allergic to poinsettias, which are another type of euphorbia, wear gloves when pruning this plant. Some people are sensitive to the milky white sap.

Features: mound-forming perennial; yellow to green, spring to mid-summer flowers; decorative foliage; fall color **Height:** 12–36"
Spread: 12–36" **Hardiness:** zones 4–10

flowering is complete, with quarter- to half-strength fertilizer. Move containers to a sheltered location protected from temperature fluctuations in winter.

Tips

Euphorbia is a neat, rounded plant that is well suited to low-maintenance and drought-tolerant containers.

Recommended

E. characias 'Glacier Blue' grows 12–18" tall and bears ice blue, cream-edged foliage and creamy white bracts with a central blue blotch. **'Tasmanian Tiger'** grows 24–36" tall and wide and has cream-edged, gray-green foliage. The flower bracts are pale yellow to creamy white with central green blotches. (Zones 6–10)

E. dulcis (sweet spurge) is a compact, upright plant. The spring flowers and bracts are yellow-green. The dark bronzy green leaves turn red or orange in fall. **'Chameleon'** has purple-red foliage that turns darker purple in fall. (Zones 4–9)

E. griffithii 'Fireglow' has light green leaves, orange stems and bright orange bracts. **'Fire Charm'** is a more compact selection. (Zones 4–9)

E. x martinii RUDOLPH ('Waleuphrud') grows 18–24" tall and wide and bears tiny, chartreuse green flowers in spring. In the coolness of fall, the plant produces red flower bracts that look like the nose of the famous reindeer. (Zones 6–10)

E. polychroma (*E. epithymoides*; cushion spurge) is a mounding, clump-forming plant. Long-lasting, yellow bracts surround the inconspicuous flowers. The foliage turns shades of purple, red or orange in fall. There are several cultivars available. **'Candy'** has purple-tinged leaves and stems. (Zones 4–9)

E. 'Shorty' is a mound-forming plant that grows 15–18" tall and wide. It has blue-green foliage whose tips turn rosy red in fall. The flower bracts are bright yellow. (Zones 6–10)

E. dulcis 'Chameleon'

False Cypress
Chamaecyparis

The evergreen foliage of false cypress provides winter color as well as solid structure for your container garden.

Growing

False cypress prefers **full sun**. The potting mix should be **neutral to acidic, moist** and **well drained**, with lots of compost mixed in. Select a large, stable container so that the plants won't tip over. Fertilize monthly during the growing season with quarter-strength

Deer seem attracted to false cypress, especially in early spring. Sprinkle the plants with red pepper flakes to discourage deer browsing.

Features: narrow, pyramidal, evergreen tree; foliage; habit; cones **Height:** 10"–6' **Spread:** 1–6' **Hardiness:** zones 4–9

fertilizer. Move containers to a sheltered location protected from the sun and wind in the colder winter areas of our states.

Avoid severe pruning because new growth will not sprout from old wood. In shaded areas, growth may be sparse or thin. Dry, brown, old leaves can be pulled from the base by hand to tidy up. Oils in the foliage of false cypress may be irritating to sensitive skin, so wearing gloves is a good option.

Tips
Tree varieties are used as specimen plants and for hedging. The dwarf and slow-growing cultivars are used in borders and rock gardens and as bonsai. False cypress shrubs can be grown near the house as evergreen specimens in large containers.

Recommended
C. lawsoniana 'Gnome' is a loosely rounded cultivar about 36" tall.

C. nootkatensis is a west coast native with pendulous growth. '**Compacta**' is a dense, rounded, compact plant with light green foliage that grows 3–6' tall and wide.

C. obtusa has foliage arranged in fan-like sprays. '**Minima**' is a dwarf, mounding cultivar. It grows about 10" tall and spreads 16" wide. '**Nana**' is a slow-growing cultivar that reaches 24–36" in height, with a slightly greater spread. '**Nana Gracilis**' is upright to broadly pyramidal, grows 3–5' tall and wide and bears dark green foliage. '**Nana Aurea**' ('Nana Lutea') is similar to 'Nana Gracilis,' except for its yellow foliage.

C. pisifera 'Nana' is a dwarf cultivar with feathery foliage. It grows into a mound about 12" in height and width.

Fan Flower

Scaevola

Fan flower's intriguing, one-sided flowers add interest to hanging baskets, planters and window boxes.

Growing

Fan flower grows well in **full sun** or **light shade**. The potting mix should be **moist** and **well drained**. Water it regularly because this plant doesn't like to dry out completely. It does, however, recover quickly from wilting when watered. Fertilize every two weeks with quarter-strength fertilizer. This plant is a perennial that is treated as an annual. Cuttings can be taken in late summer and grown indoors for use the following summer.

Tips

Fan flower is popular for hanging baskets and as an edging plant in a container where it can trail down. It is also an attractive filler plant in mixed containers because the trailing habit will spread between other plants.

Recommended

S. aemula forms a mound of foliage from which trailing stems emerge. The fan-shaped flowers come in shades of purple, usually with white bases. **'Blue Wonder'** has long, trailing branches, making it ideal for hanging baskets. It can eventually spread 36" or more. **'Saphira'** is a compact variety with deep blue flowers. WHIRLWIND BLUE is a compact plant that bears heat- and fade-resistant, blue flowers. WHIRLWIND WHITE bears white flowers on compact, heat-tolerant plants.

S. *aemula* with canna lily, verbena and others

Fan flower is native to Australia and Polynesia. Regular pinching and trimming will keep your fan flower bushy and blooming its best.

Features: decorative, bushy or trailing habit; blue, purple or white, fan-shaped flowers
Height: up to 8"   **Spread:** up to 4'
Hardiness: tender perennial grown as an annual

Flowering Maple
Abutilon

A. x *hybridum* (above & below)

Flowering maple is a vigorous shrub with beautiful flowers and decorative foliage, and it deserves a place in both your garden and your house.

Growing
Flowering maple grows well in **full sun** or **light shade**. The potting mix should be **moist** and **well drained**. Fertilize every two weeks during the growing season with quarter- to half-strength fertilizer. This tender plant must be moved indoors in winter if it is to survive. Trim it back annually to keep the size manageable.

Tips
Flowering maple makes a stunning specimen, but it is also a lovely companion plant. Plant mounding and trailing annuals around the base of flowering maple to create a pretty display for your front entryway.

Recommended
A. x *hybridum* is a bushy shrub that bears downy, maple-like leaves on woody branches. The single flowers are pendulous and bell shaped. There are a number of selections available in a variety of colors including peach, white, cream, yellow, orange, red or pink. There are also several selections with variegated foliage. Some of the variegated selections bear very few flowers. **'Kentish Belle'** bears vibrant orange flowers. **'Nabob'** has crimson red flowers.

Features: pendulous flowers in shades of yellow, peach, orange, red, pink, cream or white; maple-like, sometimes variegated foliage
Height: 4–5' **Spread:** 24–36"
Hardiness: tender shrub grown as an annual or overwintered indoors

Flowering maple is a long-lasting houseplant, providing years of enjoyment, and it will have denser growth with better foliage color and more flowers if it spends every summer enjoying the great outdoors.

Foamflower
Tiarella

Foamflower's colorful foliage mixes well with other understory plants such as hostas and ferns, and it is great for contrasting and highlighting brightly colored flowers.

Growing
Foamflower prefers **full shade, light shade** or **partial shade** with no afternoon sun. The potting mix should be **moist, slightly acidic** and **well drained**, with lots of compost and/or earthworm castings mixed in. Allow the soil to dry slightly between waterings. Fertilize once a month during the growing season with quarter- to half-strength fertilizer.

Divide in spring. Deadhead to encourage reblooming. Some foamflowers spread by runners, which are easily pulled up to stop excessive spread. If the foliage fades or rusts in summer, cut it partway to the ground, and new growth will emerge.

Tips
Use foamflower as an edging plant or filler plant in your perennial or mixed containers.

Recommended
T. **'Pirates Patch'** is a compact, mounded, slowly creeping plant with large, medium green, slightly lobed foliage centrally marked with dark burgundy. It produces a plethora of pink-tinged, white flowers. The foliage has wonderful reddish purple fall color.

T. **'Skeleton Key'** has white flowers and deeply cut, dark green, glossy foliage with purple tinges along the veins and midrib.

The starry flowers clustered along the stems look like festive sparklers.

Features: attractive and varied foliage; spring to early-summer, white or pink flowers
Height: 4–12"   **Spread:** 12–24"
Hardiness: zones 3–8

Fothergilla
Fothergilla

F. gardenii 'Blue Mist'

ragrant flowers, stunning fall color and interesting, brownish tan stems give fothergilla year-round appeal.

Growing

Fothergilla grows well in **full sun, light shade** or **partial shade**, though the best flowering and fall color occur in full sun. The potting mix should be **acidic, humus rich, moist** and **well drained**. Add compost or worm castings to the mix. Fertilize with quarter-strength fertilizer every two weeks during the growing season. Move containers to a sheltered location out of the wind and sun in winter.

Tips

Fothergilla forms a striking focal point in mixed containers. Combine it with spring-blooming plants such as tulips for early-season contrast and silver-leaved plants such as dusty miller and licorice plant for fall contrast.

Recommended

F. gardenii (dwarf fothergilla) is a bushy shrub. The dark green leaves turn brilliant, mixed shades of yellow, orange and red in fall. Bottlebrush-shaped flowers are produced in spring and have a delicate honey fragrance. **'Blue Mist'** has blue-green foliage that is pretty in summer, but it doesn't develop brilliant fall color like the species does.

F. major (large fothergilla) is very similar in appearance to dwarf fothergilla, but it is not as suitable for container culture because it grows at least twice as large.

Features: bushy shrub; attractive foliage; good fall color; fragrant, white, spring flowers
Height: 24–36"   **Spread:** 24–36"
Hardiness: zones 4–8

Fuchsia
Fuchsia

F. x *hybrida* 'Gartenmeister Bonstedt'

$\mathcal{T}$he cool summer areas of the Pacific Northwest are a perfect climate for growing fuchsias. These plants are our reward for putting up with cloudy summer days.

Growing

Fuchsias grow best in **partial shade** or **light shade**. They are generally not tolerant of summer heat, and full sun can be too hot for them. The potting mix should be **moist** and **well drained**.

Fuchsias bloom on new growth, which will be stimulated by a high-nitrogen plant food.

Features: pink, orange, red, purple or white, often bicolored flowers; attractive foliage
Height: 6"–6' **Spread:** 6–36"
Hardiness: zones 6–9; tender shrub grown as an annual

Fertilize bi-weekly during the growing season with half-strength fertilizer. Fuchsias should be deadheaded. Pluck the swollen seedpods from behind the fading petals.

Tender fuchsias can be overwintered indoors or thrown away at the end of the season. Many hardy fuchsias will overwinter near the coast. Don't prune off the dead branches until you see new growth coming from soil level.

Tips

Upright fuchsias can be used in mixed containers. Pendulous fuchsias are most often used in hanging baskets, but also look great spilling over the edge of a large container. Hardy fuchsias can be the focal point of large container gardens, but they are slow to get started in spring. Pair them with early-blooming pansies, creeping evergreen euonymus or dwarf rhododendrons and azaleas.

Recommended

F. **Angels' Earrings Series** from Proven Winners are very heat and humidity tolerant plants, growing 10–12" tall.

F. **x** *hybrida* offers dozens of wonderful hybrids. The upright selections grow 18–36" tall, and the pendulous fuchsias grow 6–24" tall. **'Gartenmeister Bonstedt'** is an upright cultivar that grows about 24" tall and bears tubular, orange-red flowers. The foliage is bronzy red with purple undersides.

F. *magellanica* (hardy fuchsia) is an upright, bushy shrub that grows 4–6' tall and 24–36" wide in containers. It blooms from late spring to the first frost in fall. **'Aurea'** is a low, spreading plant that bears red flowers and yellow-green foliage that can take on purple highlights in fall.

F. x hybrida cultivar

Geranium
Pelargonium

P. peltatum cultivar with lobelia

Geraniums are perhaps the quintessential container plants, and for good reason—they perform exceptionally well in containers. There are a wide variety of geraniums available, and they grow well with many other plants, so one need not plant the classic zonal geranium/spike/vinca combination. Try the scented geraniums for their uniquely decorative and wonderfully fragrant foliage as well as for their flowers.

Growing
Geraniums prefer **full sun** but tolerate partial shade, although they may not bloom as profusely. The potting mix should be **well drained**. Fertilize with quarter-strength fertilizer every one or two weeks during the growing season. Deadhead to keep geraniums blooming and looking neat, and pinch them back occasionally to keep plants bushy.

Geraniums are perennials that are treated as annuals. They can be kept

Features: decorative, often colorful foliage; red, pink, violet, orange, salmon, white or purple, summer flowers   **Height:** 8–24"
Spread: 6"–4'   **Hardiness:** tender perennial grown as an annual

P. peltatum with portulaca in planter and petunias (above), *P. peltatum* cultivar with jasmine and bacopa (below)

indoors over winter in a bright room. You can also overwinter geraniums by putting them in a protected, frost-free garden shed, garage or basement and keeping the soil very dry. Begin to water in March and then fertilize in April just before bringing the plants back outdoors after all danger of frost has passed in May.

Tips

With their brightly colored flowers and decorative foliage, geraniums are very popular for mixed containers, window boxes and hanging baskets.

Recommended

P. capitatum is a compact plant with irregularly shaped, rose-scented leaves. It bears pinkish purple flowers.

***P.* 'Chocolate Peppermint'** has green leaves with irregular, bronze-purple centers that smell like chocolatey peppermint. The flowers are pink and white.

P. crispum (lemon-scented geranium) forms a compact, low or upright mound of bright green, crinkly, lemon-scented foliage. It bears small, pink flowers in summer. **'Cream Peach'** has green, cream and yellow variegated, peach-scented foliage. **'Variegatum'** ('Variegated Prince Rupert') has ruffled, cream variegated, lemon-scented foliage.

P.* x *hortorum (zonal geranium) is a bushy plant with red, pink, purple, orange or white flowers and frequently banded or multi-colored foliage. The **Fireworks Collection** includes several cultivars with star-shaped flowers in several shades including red and pink. The maple leaf–shaped foliage is colorfully banded. Plants have a compact habit.

P. peltatum (ivy-leaved geranium) has thick, waxy leaves and a trailing habit. It bears loose clusters of colorful flowers. Many cultivars are available.

Glory Bush
Tibouchina

T. urvilleana

Glory bush is a wonderful, colorful accent plant that will give a tropical look to your containers.

Growing

Glory bush grows best in **full sun** in a sheltered location. The potting mix should be **slightly acidic, moist** and **well drained**. Fertilize every two weeks during the growing season with quarter- to half-strength fertilizer. This tender plant should be over-wintered indoors in a sunny room. It may survive outdoors in zone 9 if given adequate frost protection.

Tips

Glory bush is useful as a specimen or as an accent in a mixed container. It can be trained into a small tree. The velvety leaves provide an attractive backdrop for red or orange flowers.

Recommended

T. urvilleana is a fast-growing, upright to rounded shrub. The dark green, velvety leaves may have red margins, and older foliage may be marked and spotted yellow, orange and red. Fat, rounded, red-tinged buds open to reveal vivid, royal purple flowers in late spring to late fall.

Also called: princess flower, pleroma, Brazilian spider flower   **Features:** bushy, erect to rounded, evergreen shrub; purple flowers; dark green, velvety foliage   **Height:** 5–10'   **Spread:** 5–10'   **Hardiness:** zones 10–11; tender shrub grown as an annual or overwintered indoors

Golden Hakone Grass

Hakonechloa

H. macra 'Aureola' with ligularia, begonia and lysimachia

Golden hakone grass is an attractive, shade-loving grass that provides interest throughout the growing season.

Growing
Golden hakone grass grows well in **light shade** or **partial shade**. The potting mix should be **moist** and **well drained**. Fertilize every two weeks during the growing season with quarter- to half-strength fertilizer. Where it is hardy, move the container to a sheltered location out of the wind and sun where it will be protected from temperature fluctuations in winter. Where it is not hardy, it can be cut back and overwintered in an unheated shed or garage.

Tips
Golden hakone grass is one of the few grasses that grow well in shaded locations. Its texture and color are a good contrast to broad-leaved shade plants such as hosta and lungwort. This grass creates a striking display spilling over the sides of containers. It looks lovely paired with red Japanese maple trees in a large pot.

Recommended
H. macra forms a clump of bright green, arching, grass-like foliage that turns deep pink in fall, then bronze as winter sets in. Several cultivars are available. **'All Gold'** has pure gold leaves and is more upright and spiky in habit. **'Aureola'** has bright yellow foliage with narrow, green streaks; the foliage turns pink in fall.

Also called: Japanese forest grass
Features: perennial grass; arching habit; fall color   **Height:** 12–24"   **Spread:** 12–24"
Hardiness: zones 5–8

This ornamental grass is native to Japan, where it grows on mountainsides and cliffs, often near streams and other water sources.

Golden Marguerite
Anthemis

Pretty, daisy-like flowers almost completely cover the fine, feathery foliage when these plants are in bloom.

Growing

Golden marguerite grows best in **full sun**. The potting mix should be **well drained**. This plant is drought tolerant. Fertilize monthly during the growing season with quarter-strength fertlizer. Move hardy plants to a sheltered location in winter. Where they are not hardy, store containers in a shed or garage in winter.

Tips

Golden marguerite can be planted alone in specimen containers and is also a cheerful addition to mixed containers. The daisy-like flowers have a warm, welcoming appearance that makes them a good choice for containers placed near an entryway.

Recommended

A. marshalliana (marshall chamomile) is a low, mound-forming plant. Its finely divided leaves are covered in long, silvery hairs. Bright golden yellow flowers are borne in summer.

A. punctata subsp. *cupaniana* forms a low mat of silvery gray foliage. It bears yellow-centered, white flowers in early summer. (Zones 6–8)

A. tinctoria (golden marguerite) forms a mounded clump of foliage that is completely covered in bright or pale yellow, daisy-like flowers in summer. **'Charme'** is a compact plant that grows 12–16" tall and 12" wide with bright yellow flowers. **'Grallach Gold'** bears bright golden yellow flowers. **'Moonlight'** bears large, buttery or pale yellow flowers.

A. tinctoria

Shear plants back as flowering finishes to encourage fresh growth and a second flush of flowers.

Also called: marguerite daisy **Features:** mounding or spreading perennial; yellow, orange or cream, daisy-like, summer flowers; finely divided or feathery foliage
Height: 8–36" **Spread:** 12–36"
Hardiness: zones 3–8

Hardy Geranium
Geranium

G. JOLLY BEE, a Proven Winners Selection

Hardy geraniums are available in a huge range of heights and colors, at least some of which are sure to suit your container garden needs.

Also called: cranesbill **Features:** clump- or mound-forming perennial; white, red, pink, purple or blue, summer flowers; dense, often deeply divided foliage **Height:** 6–36" **Spread:** 12–36" **Hardiness:** zones 3–8

Growing

Hardy geraniums prefer to grow in **partial shade** or **light shade** but tolerate full sun. The potting mix should be **well drained**. Fertilize every two weeks during the growing season with quarter-strength fertilizer. Move containers to a sheltered location protected from temperature fluctuations in winter. Be prepared to prune this robust plant, or it will overtake the other plants in the pot.

Tips

These long-flowering plants are great in mixed containers. The simple flowers aren't exceptionally showy, but their constant presence is appreciated as other flowers come and go.

Recommended

G. 'Johnson's Blue' forms a spreading mat of foliage. Bright blue flowers are borne over a long period in summer.

G. JOLLY BEE is a vigorous, mounding plant with large, violet-blue flowers that bloom for an extended period in summer and have orange to red fall color.

G. macrorrhizum (bigroot cranesbill) forms a spreading mound of fragrant foliage. This plant is quite drought tolerant. Flowers in variable shades of pink are borne in spring and early summer.

G. x *oxonianum* is a vigorous, mound-forming plant with attractive, evergreen foliage. It bears pink flowers from spring to fall.

G. pratense (meadow cranesbill) forms an upright clump and bears clusters of white, blue or light purple flowers for a short period in early summer. It self-seeds freely. 'Plenum Violaceum' bears purple, double flowers for a longer period than the species.

G. sanguineum (bloody cranesbill, bloodred cranesbill) forms a dense, mounding clump and bears bright magenta flowers mostly in early summer and sporadically until fall. 'Elsbeth' has light pink flowers with dark pink veins and bright red fall foliage. 'Shepherd's Warning' grows 6" tall and bears rosy pink flowers. Var. *striatum* is heat and drought tolerant. It has pale pink blooms with blood red veins.

The decorative foliage of many hardy geraniums is reason enough to grow them.

G. 'Johnson's Blue' (above)
G. *pratense* 'Plenum Violaceum' (below)

Hebe
Hebe

Generally, small-leaved hebes are hardier than large-leaved hebes. Hebe trials at the North Willamette Research Station are determining cold hardiness for a large number of hebe species and hybrids.

Hebes are attractive, low-maintenance shrubs that are wonderful container garden plants, especially west of the Cascades.

Growing
Hebes grow well in **full sun to partial shade** in a sheltered location. The potting mix should be **neutral to alkaline, moist** and **very well drained**. Fertilize once a month during the growing season with quarter- to half-strength fertilizer. Hebe is tolerant of urban pollution.

Many hebes will survive the winters in western Washington and Oregon. Where plants aren't hardy, move them to a cool, bright room indoors in winter. Plants may be damaged by early fall or late spring frost.

Features: tender, mound-forming, evergreen shrub; dense, attractive foliage; purple, red, pink, blue or white, fragrant flowers
Height: 8"–5'   **Spread:** 2–5'
Hardiness: zones 8–10

Most hebes need little or no pruning. Large-leaf hebes benefit from removing the spent flower spikes. Leggy or neglected plants, or plants damaged by a hard winter, can be cut back hard to 6–12" above the soil in spring.

Tips

Hebes can be planted with annuals and perennials in mixed containers and are also excellent as specimens. They make wonderful evergreen shrubs for a mixed container that you want to look good even in winter.

Recommended

H. buxifolia (box-leaf hebe) grows 3–4' tall and wide. It has small, bright green, boxwood-like foliage and bears small spikes of white flowers in early summer.

H. cupressoides is a whipcord hebe that forms a dense, upright mound of small, scale-like foliage that closely resembles cypress foliage. The plant grows 3–4' tall and wide and bears lilac flowers that fade to white. **'Boughton Dome'** forms a dense mound 12" tall and 24" wide.

H. pinguifolia **'Pagei'** is a low-growing groundcover that roots at the nodes. It grows about 8–12" tall and 4–5' wide, bearing small, blue-gray leaves and white, summer flowers.

H. **'Red Edge'** is a compact plant that bears blue-green foliage with thin, red margins. The leaves are tinged red when young. It grows about 18" tall and 24" wide, producing lilac blooms that fade to white in summer.

Heliotrope
Heliotropium

H. arborescens ATLANTIS with angelonia, lobelia, sweet flag, licorice plant and sage

Heliotrope's big clusters of fragrant flowers on bushy plants have renewed the popularity of this old-fashioned favorite.

Growing
Heliotrope grows best in **full sun**. The potting mix should be **humus rich, moist** and **well drained**. Fertilize once a month during the growing season with quarter-strength fertilizer. Plants can be treated as houseplants in winter; keep them in a cool and sunny location indoors. This plant is very attractive to slugs and snails. Pick them off as soon as you spot them.

Tips
Heliotrope is ideal for growing in containers placed where the wonderful scent of the flowers can be enjoyed. Combine purple-flowered heliotrope with yellow- or white-flowered plants and plants with burgundy foliage for striking color contrasts.

Recommended
H. arborescens is a low, bushy shrub that bears large clusters of sweet-scented, purple flowers all summer. Some new cultivars are not as strongly scented as the species. ATLANTIS, a Proven Selection by Proven Winners, is heat-tolerant and bears large, fragrant clusters of royal purple flowers. **'Black Beauty'** bears deep purple, fragrant flowers. **'Blue Wonder'** is a compact plant with heavily scented, dark purple flowers.

These old-fashioned flowers may have been popular in your grandmother's garden. Their recent comeback is no surprise, considering their attractive foliage, flowers and scent.

Also called: cherry pie plant **Features:** bushy habit; purple or white, fragrant flowers; attractive foliage **Height:** 8–24" **Spread:** 12–24" **Hardiness:** tender shrub grown as an annual or overwintered indoors

Hens and Chicks

Sempervivum

Hens and chicks are easy to grow. They need little care other than a very well-drained soil and a light sprinkle of water during extended dry periods.

Growing

Hens and chicks grow well in **full sun** or **partial shade**. The potting mix should be **very well drained**. Add fine gravel or grit to the mix to provide adequate drainage. Fertilize once or twice during the growing season with quarter-strength fertilizer.

Tips

These plants can be used in shallow troughs and make interesting center-pieces on patio and picnic tables. They can also be combined with other drought-tolerant plants, such as sedum and yarrow, in mixed containers. Creative container gardeners enjoy growing these succulents in old shoes, boots, metal toy dump trucks and just about any other container with drainage holes.

Recommended

S. tectorum is one of the most commonly grown hens and chicks of the many species, cultivars and hybrids available. It forms a low-growing mat of fleshy-leaved rosettes. Small, new rosettes are quickly produced and grow and multiply to fill almost any space. Flowers may be produced in summer. **'Atropurpureum'** has dark reddish purple leaves. **'Limelight'** has yellow-green, pink-tipped foliage. **'Pacific Hawk'** has dark red leaves that are edged with silvery hairs.

S. arachnoideum (cobweb houseleek) is identical to *S. tectorum* except that the tips of the leaves are entwined with hairy fibers, giving the appearance of cobwebs. This plant may need protection during wet weather.

S. tectorum with phormium

These curious plants can grow on almost any surface. In the past, they were grown on tile roofs—it was believed they would protect the house from lightning.

Also called: houseleek **Features:** rosette-forming, succulent perennial; red, yellow, white or purple flowers **Height:** 2–6" **Spread:** 12" or more **Hardiness:** zones 3–8

Hosta

Hosta

H. cultivar with others

○f you have a covered entryway so shaded that few flowers will bloom, place a pair of potted hostas on either side of the door for a dramatic and refreshing welcome.

Features: clump-forming perennial; decorative foliage in shades of green or variegated with yellow or cream; late-summer or fall, mauve, purple or white flowers **Height:** 1–4' **Spread:** 18–36" **Hardiness:** zones 3–8

Growing

Hostas prefer **light shade** or **partial shade** but will grow in full shade. Some will tolerate full sun. The potting mix should be **moist** and **well drained**. Fertilize monthly during the growing season with half-strength fertilizer. Move containers to a sheltered location in winter.

Hostas can grow in the same pot for many years without needing a transplant, but as the roots become more crowded, the leaves will become smaller and the plants will require more water.

Tips

Hostas are wonderful woodland plants and look very attractive when combined with ferns and other fine-textured plants, especially in dark or rustic containers. Combine a variety of hostas together or mix them with other plants.

Recommended

Hostas have been subjected to a great deal of crossbreeding and hybridizing, resulting in hundreds of cultivars. There are almost endless variations in hosta foliage; swirls, stripes, puckers and ribs enhance the leaves' various sizes, shapes and colors. **'Baby Bunting'** is a popular cultivar with dark green to slightly bluish green, heart-shaped leaves and light purple flowers. **'Fragrant Bouquet'** has bright green leaves with creamy yellow margins and very fragrant, white flowers. **'Gold Standard'** is a hosta fancier's favorite, bearing bright yellow leaves with narrow, green margins. **'Guacamole'** has chartreuse leaves with dark green margins and fragrant, white flowers. **'June'** has bright yellow leaves with blue-green margins and light purple flowers. **'Pandora's Box'** forms a compact mound of creamy leaves with irregular green margins and bears light purple flowers. **'Tardiflora'** forms an attractive, small mound of dark green leaves and bears lots of light purple flowers in fall.

Choosing containers that are proportionate to the mature size of your hostas is of prime importance if you are planning to overwinter them for more than one year. It is wise to learn the mature size of the hosta, then select your container based on that information.

H. fortuneii 'Francee' (above), *H.* cultivar (center)

H. cultivar with coral bells and barberry (below)

Hydrangea
Hydrangea

Proven Winners Selection *H. paniculata* LIMELIGHT

From rounded shrubs and small trees to climbing vines, hydrangeas offer a wealth of possibilities for use in containers.

Features: mounding, spreading or climbing, deciduous shrub or tree; clusters of white, pink, blue, purple or red flowers in summer; attractive foliage, sometimes with good fall color; some with exfoliating bark **Height:** 3–10' **Spread:** 3–10' **Hardiness:** zones 3–8

Growing

Hydrangeas grow well in **full sun** or **partial shade**, and some species tolerate full shade. These plants perform best in cool, moist conditions, and some shade will reduce leaf and flower scorch in hotter gardens. The potting mix should be **humus rich, moist** and **well drained**. Fertilize monthly during the growing season with quarter- to half-strength fertilizer. Move containers to a sheltered location out of the wind and sun in winter.

Tips

Hydrangeas can really brighten up your mixed containers with their large flower clusters. Shrubby forms can be grown alone or combined with other plants. Tree forms are small enough to grow in containers but large enough to offer a good vertical accent. Climbing hydrangea can be used to create a beautiful display against a wall or over the edge of a balcony.

Recommended

H. anomala subsp. *petiolaris* (climbing hydrangea) is an elegant climbing plant with dark green, glossy leaves. It bears clusters of lacy-looking flowers in midsummer. Unlike most hydrangeas, this climber needs at least half a day of sun to bloom. (Zones 4–8)

H. arborescens **'Annabelle'** (Annabelle hydrangea) is a rounded shrub that bears large clusters of white flowers, even in shady conditions.

H. macrophylla (above & below)

H. macrophylla (bigleaf hydrangea) is a rounded shrub that bears flowers in shades of pink, red, blue or purple from mid- to late summer. The acidity of the planting mix affects the color of the blooms. The pH of most mixes will yield pink flowers. Make the soil more acidic if you want blue flowers. ENDLESS SUMMER bears deep pink, mophead flower clusters over a long season on current and prior-year growth. It can be pruned any time and not suffer from a lack of flowers the following year. It is quite toleratant of cold winters and late spring frosts. (Zones 5–8)

H. quercifolia (oakleaf hydrangea) is a mound-forming shrub with attractive, cinnamon brown, exfoliating bark. Its beautiful, large, leathery leaves are lobed like an oak's and turn bronze to bright red in fall. It bears conical clusters of sterile as well as fertile flowers. (Zones 4–8)

Hyssop
Agastache

A. foeniculum

The leaves of anise hyssop can be diffused in hot water for tea.

Features: bushy, upright perennial; mint or licorice-scented foliage; pink, purple, purple-blue or orange flowers **Height:** 12–36" **Spread:** 12–36" **Hardiness:** zones 2–10

This perennial is a favorite with hummingbirds, butterflies and other pollinators.

Growing
Hyssop grows well in **full sun** or **partial shade**. The potting mix should be **well drained**. Fertilize every two weeks during the growing season with quarter-strength fertilizer. Deadheading will keep plants neat and encourage continued blooming. Tender selections will have to be overwintered indoors or replaced each year. Hardy selections can be kept in a sheltered spot outdoors in winter.

Tips
These bushy plants make good companions in mixed containers. Combine them with lavender, scented-leaf geranium, lilac and thyme for a fragrance-themed container that is sure to attract pollinators to your garden.

Recommended
A. aurantiaca is a bushy, upright plant with gray-green, mint-scented leaves. It bears spikes of orange-pink flowers in summer. 'Apricot Sprite' bears lots of apricot orange flowers. (Zones 7–10)

A. 'Firebird' has irregular, bronzy maroon markings on its leaves and bears spikes of coppery orange flowers in summer. (Zones 6–10)

A. foeniculum (anise hyssop) is a bushy, upright, anise-scented perennial with slightly downy leaves and dense spikes of lilac blue flowers. 'Snow Spike' has white flowers.

Impatiens
Impatiens

*I*mpatiens, with their brightly colored flowers, are just as valuable in shady containers as they are in shady ground-based gardens.

Growing
Impatiens do best in **partial shade** or **light shade** but tolerate full shade or, if kept moist, full sun. New Guinea impatiens are best adapted to sunny locations, but the foliage may still scorch in the hot afternoon sun. The potting mix should be **humus rich, moist** and **well drained**. Mix in some compost or earthworm castings. Fertilize every two weeks with quarter-strength fertilizer.

Tips
These bushy or spreading plants make great colorful fillers in shady containers. Choose impatiens for the contrast or complement their flowers can create with the other plants in your containers. Combine impatiens with begonia and lobelia in shades of white and yellow to light up a deeply shaded area.

Recommended
I. hawkeri (New Guinea Group, New Guinea impatiens) are bushy plants with glossy, dark green foliage that is often variegated with a yellow stripe down the center. The flowers come in shades of red, orange, pink, purple or white. Cultivars are available.

I. walleriana (busy Lizzie) is a bushy, spreading plant with glossy leaves in shades of light through dark green or bronze. The flowers come in shades of purple, red, burgundy, pink, orange, salmon, apricot, yellow, white or bicolored. Many cultivars are available.

I. walleriana with baby tears and vinca

The name Impatiens *refers to the impatient nature of the seedpods. When ripe, the seedpods burst open with the slightest touch and scatter their seeds.*

Features: bushy or spreading habit; flowers in shades of purple, red, burgundy, pink, orange, salmon, apricot, yellow, white or bicolored **Height:** 6–18" **Spread:** 8–24" **Hardiness:** tender annual

Iris

Iris

Iris with others

rises are valuable both for their strap-like foliage and their beautiful, colorful flowers.

Growing

Irises grow best in **full sun** but tolerate partial shade or light shade. The potting mix should be **moist** and **well drained**, though several species tolerate dry conditions. Fertilize monthly during the growing season with quarter-strength fertilizer. Move containers to a sheltered location out of the wind and sun in winter.

Tips

Irises provide a wonderful strong, vertical accent. Several species grow in wet soil and can be combined with other moisture-lovers such as cardinal flower and elephant ears for a bog-themed container. There are iris flowers in almost every imaginable shade, and these can be used to create complementary or contrasting combinations in mixed containers.

Recommended

I. ensata (Japanese iris) is a water-loving species that bears blue, purple, pink or white flowers in early to mid-summer.

I. germanica **hybrids** (German iris, bearded iris) are drought-tolerant plants that bear the most decorative flowers in every imaginable color.

Irises are steeped in history and lore. The name Iris *comes from the Greek messenger to the gods, who travelled using the rainbow as a bridge.*

Features: clump-forming, rhizomatous perennial; narrow or broad, strap-like, possibly variegated foliage; summer flowers in every shade of the rainbow **Height:** 1–4' **Spread:** 8–36" **Hardiness:** zones 2–8

I. pallida (sweet iris, variegated iris) is a drought-tolerant, purple-flowered species that is rarely grown, but its variegated cultivars are a useful addition to mixed containers. **'Argentea Variegata'** has cream-and-green-striped foliage. **'Aurea Variegata'** has yellow-and-green-striped foliage.

I. pseudacorus (yellow flag iris) is a moisture-loving species with narrow foliage and bright yellow, brown- or purple-marked flowers in mid- and late summer.

I. sibirica (Siberian iris) likes a moist but well-drained soil. It bears purple flowers in early summer, though cultivars with pink, blue, white, yellow or red flowers are available.

I. versicolor (blue flag iris) is a moisture-loving species that bears flowers in varied shades of purple in early summer.

I. germanica 'Stepping Out' (above), *I. pseudacorus* (below)

Japanese Painted Fern
Athyrium

A. niponicum 'Silver Falls'

The demand for these wonderful ferns will certainly encourage enthusiastic breeders to create more varieties.

Features: deciduous, perennial fern; decorative foliage **Height:** 1–4' **Spread:** 1–4' **Hardiness:** zones 4–8

Delicate, decorative and well behaved: *Athyrium* is one of the few fern genera really suitable for container culture.

Growing
This fern grows well in **full shade, partial shade** or **light shade**. The potting mix should be **acidic** and **moist**. Fertilize every two weeks during the growing season with quarter-strength fertilizer. It will need some protection in winter.

Cover it if it will be left outdoors, or move it to a sheltered location.

Tips

These ferns make an attractive addition to almost any mixed planter. Create a woodland understory in a pot. Combine hosta, coral bells, Annabelle hydrangea and either *Athyrium* species in a large planter for a shaded location. Try combining the gray foliage of dusty miller or licorice plant with pots of Japanese painted fern to bring out the silver highlights on the leaves. This colorful fern also looks great in a sleek metallic pot for a contemporary container garden.

Recommended

A. felix-femina (lady fern) forms a dense clump of lacy fronds. The appearance can be quite variable, as the leaflets on the fronds and the fronds themselves are prone to dividing, giving the plants a more lacy appearance or sometimes even a dense, ball-like appearance. It varies in size from dwarfs that grow 12" tall and wide to larger plants that can grow 2–4' tall and wide. Interesting cultivars include **'Dre's Dagger,'** with narrow leaflets arranged in four rows around each frond, and **'Encourage,'** whose leaflets are divided at the tips, giving a frilly or fan-like appearance to the outer edges of each frond. Somewhat harder to find, but interesting nonetheless, is **'Acrocladon,'** whose fronds subdivide so often that the fern appears to be a small, dense ball of foliage.

A. niponicum var. *pictum* (Japanese painted fern) is a low, creeping fern with reddish to burgundy stems and a silvery metallic sheen to the bronzy fronds. Several cultivars have been developed with varied frond colors. **'Burgundy Lace'** has pinkish purple fronds with a metallic sheen. **'Silver Falls'** has silvery metallic fronds with striking, reddish purple stems and veins.

A. niponicum var. *pictum* with iris, heucherella and others (above), *A. felix-femina* (below)

Kalanchoe

Kalanchoe

K. blossfeldiana

Kalanchoe is an extremely varied group of plants. There are fuzzy ones, waxy ones, cascading ones and upright ones; some have decorative foliage, others are grown strictly for flowers.

Growing

Kalanchoes grow best in **light shade** or **partial shade** with protection from the hot afternoon sun. The potting mix should be **well drained**. Fertilize monthly during the growing season with half-strength fertilizer. Plants can be moved indoors and treated as houseplants at the end of summer.

Features: colorful flowers; glossy or fuzzy, succulent foliage   **Height:** 6–18"   **Spread:** 10–18"   **Hardiness:** tender perennial grown as an annual

Tips

Kalanchoes are interesting accent plants that add a touch of the unusual to your mixed containers. Their drought tolerance makes them useful for gardeners who occasionally forget to water.

Recommended

K. blossfeldiana (flaming katy) is a bushy, upright plant with rounded, fleshy leaves with scalloped edges. The flowers are borne in large clusters in colors such as yellow, peach, red, white or pink.

K. tomentosa (panda plant, pussy ears) is a bushy, upright plant with gray-green leaves that are covered in short, silvery hairs. The tips and margins are marked with brown.

Lady's Mantle
Alchemilla

Few other perennials look as captivating as lady's mantle does with droplets of morning dew clinging like shimmering pearls to its velvety leaves.

Growing
Lady's mantle grows well in **light shade** or **partial shade** with protection from the afternoon sun. Hot locations and excessive sun will scorch the leaves. The potting mix should be **humus rich, moist** and **well drained**. Fertilize every two weeks during the growing season with quarter-strength fertilizer. Leaves can be sheared back in summer if they begin to look tired and heat stressed; new leaves will emerge. Move containers to a sheltered location where they will be protected from temperature fluctuations in winter.

Tips
Lady's mantle is ideal for mixed containers, where it has a visually softening effect. Combine it with yellow- and purple-flowered annuals for an elegant, contrasting combination.

Recommended
A. alpina (alpine lady's mantle) is a low-growing plant that reaches 3–5" tall and spreads about 20". Clusters of tiny, yellow flowers are borne in summer.

A. mollis (common lady's mantle) forms a mound of soft, rounded foliage and produces sprays of frothy-looking, yellowish green flowers in early summer. It grows 8–18" tall and spreads about 24".

A. mollis

The chartreuse yellow flower sprays make interesting substitutes for baby's breath in fresh and dried arrangements.

Features: mound-forming perennial; yellow or yellow-green, summer and early fall flowers; attractive, downy foliage
Height: 2–18" **Spread:** 18–24"
Hardiness: zones 3–8

Lamium

Lamium

L. *maculatum* 'White Nancy,' a Proven Winners
Selection, with others

*Lamium is usually quite invasive in the
ground. Growing it in containers keeps it
from spreading out of control.*

Features: spreading or trailing perennial;
decorative, variegated foliage; pink, white,
yellow or purple, small, summer flowers
Height: 6–12"   **Spread:** 12–24"
Hardiness: zones 2–8

hese plants, with their striped, dotted or banded, silver and green
foliage provide a summer-long attrac-
tion and thrive on the barest neccessi-
ties of life.

Growing

Lamium grows well in **light shade** or
partial shade with protection from the
hot afternoon sun. The potting mix
should be **moist** and **well drained**. Fertilize no more than once a month

during the growing season with quarter-strength fertilizer. Move containers to a sheltered location in winter where they will be protected from temperature fluctuations.

Tips

Lamium is a stunning foliage plant, and its spreading nature makes it a fantastic filler plant in mixed containers. It will trail over the edges of containers and hanging baskets. Try it with other colorful foliage plants such as foamflower, coral bells and any grasses.

Recommended

L. galeobdolon (*Lamiastrum galeobdolon*; yellow archangel, false lamium) is a mounding, spreading plant with silver-marked leaves and short spikes of yellow flowers in summer. This is a very invasive evergreen perennial in shaded gardens. Don't let it escape from the pot, or it could root and smother your house and garden. **'Florentium'** ('Variegatum') is a low-growing cultivar with silvery leaves edged in green. **'Hermann's Pride'** forms a dense mat of white-speckled leaves. **'Silver Angel'** is a spreading plant with silvery foliage. (Zones 3–8)

L. maculatum (spotted dead nettle) is a low-growing, spreading plant with green leaves with white or silvery markings. It bears short spikes of pink, white or mauve flowers in summer. **'Anne Greenaway'** has silver, green and yellow variegated leaves and lavender flowers. **'Aureum'** has variegated chartreuse and silver foliage and pink flowers. **'Beacon Silver'** has silvery leaves with dark green margins and pink flowers. **'Orchid Frost'** has silvery foliage edged in blue-green and bears deep pink blooms. **'White Nancy,'** a Proven Selection by Proven Winners, has silvery white foliage and white flowers.

L. galeobdolon 'Florentium' with others (above)
L. maculatum 'Beacon Silver' with impatiens (below)

Lavender
Lavandula

L. angustifolia

The soil near the coast may be too acidic or too poorly drained to grow lavender in the ground. Growing lavender in a container is the practical solution.

Features: bushy, woody shrub; narrow, gray-green leaves; purple, pink or blue, mid-summer to fall flowers   **Height:** 8–24"
Spread: 12–24"   **Hardiness:** zones 5–8

Lavender is a beautiful, aromatic plant that is a welcome addition to sunny container gardens.

Growing
Lavender grows best in **full sun**. The potting mix should be **alkaline** and **well drained**. Established plants tolerate heat and drought. Mulch the soil with white oyster shells or white pebbles to help reflect heat and light onto these sun-loving perennials. Fertilize monthly during the growing season with quarter-strength fertilizer. Move containers to a sheltered location and cover them, or move them to an unheated shed or garage, in winter.

Tips
Lavender makes a good shrubby addition to mixed containers. Good companions for it include other drought-tolerant specimens such as thyme and sedum.

Recommended
L. angustifolia (English lavender) is an aromatic, bushy shrub often treated as a perennial. From mid-summer to fall, it bears spikes of small flowers in varied shades of purple. **'Hidcote'** ('Hidcote Blue') bears spikes of deep purple flowers. **'Jean Davis'** is a compact cultivar with spikes of pale pink flowers. **'Lady'** bears purple flowers and can be grown from seed to flower the first summer.

L. x *intermedia* is a rounded shrub with aromatic, gray-green leaves and spikes of blue or purple flowers held on long stems.

L. stoechas (French lavender) is a compact, bushy shrub with gray-green leaves and dark purple flower spikes. **'Kew Red'** bears bright pink flowers with light pink bracts. (Zone 8)

Licorice Plant
Helichrysum

The silvery sheen of licorice plant, caused by a fine, soft pubescence on its leaves, makes it a perfect complement for many other plants.

Growing
Licorice plant prefers **full sun**. The potting mix should be **neutral to alkaline** and **well drained**. Licorice plant wilts if the soil dries out but revives quickly once watered. It is easy to start more plants from cuttings in fall, giving you a supply of new plants for the following spring. Once they have rooted, keep the young plants in a cool, bright room during winter.

Tips
Include licorice plant in your hanging baskets and container plantings, and the trailing growth will quickly fill in and provide a soft, silvery setting for the colorful flowers of other plants as it cascades over the edges.

Recommended
H. petiolare is a trailing plant with fuzzy, gray-green leaves. The cultivars are more common than the species. The gray-leaved varieties grow faster than the variegated and green-leaved varieties. **'Crispum'** has small leaves with rippled edges. **'Lemon Licorice'** has yellow-green foliage. **'Licorice Splash'** has gray-green leaves with irregular, creamy margins. **'Limelight'** has bright lime green leaves. **'Petite Licorice'** is a compact selection with small, gray-green leaves. **'Silver'** has gray-green leaves covered in a silvery white down. **'White Licorice'** has silvery white foliage.

H. petiolare 'Petite Licorice' with dusty miller

This plant is a good indicator plant for hanging baskets. When you see licorice plant wilting, it is time to get out the hose or watering can.

Features: bushy or trailing habit; downy, gray-green, silvery, yellow or cream and green variegated foliage **Height:** 6–24" **Spread:** 1–4' **Hardiness:** tender shrub or perennial grown as an annual

Lilac
Syringa

S. x *hyacinthiflora* 'Evangeline'

Lilacs are frost-loving shrubs that bloom very well in Spokane and east of the Cascades, areas that receive less rain than near the coast. Rainy weather makes lilacs more susceptible to leaf blights.

Features: rounded or suckering, deciduous shrub or small tree with attractive, late-spring to mid-summer flowers   **Height:** 3–15'
Spread: 3–15'   **Hardiness:** zones 3–8

Even for container gardeners, the hardest thing about growing lilacs is choosing from the many species and hundreds of cultivars available.

Growing
Lilacs grow best in **full sun**. The potting mix should be **humus rich** and **well drained**. Fertilize monthly during the growing season with quarter-strength fertilizer. Lilacs are among the hardiest of plants. Move containers to a location out of the sun and wind, and they should make it through just about anything winter can throw at them.

Tips
Lilacs make lovely vertical accents and are good structural plants for large containers. Most can be trained into a tree form and can be grown in a container for several years before they become too large and need to be transplanted into a garden.

Recommended
S. x *hyacinthiflora* hybrids are hardy, upright, disease-resistant shrubs that spread with age. They bear clusters of fragrant flowers in mid- to late spring. The leaves turn reddish purple in fall.

S. meyeri is a compact, rounded shrub that bears pink or lavender, fragrant flowers. '**Palibin**' is a slow-growing cultivar with pinkish purple flowers. '**Tinkerbelle**' bears deep pink flowers.

S. patula '**Miss Kim**' is a vigorous, compact lilac with pale purple flower buds that open lavender blue. It has attractive, dark green foliage.

Lilyturf

Liriope

L. muscari 'Monroe White'

Resistant to drought, heat, humidity and most pests and diseases, lilyturf is one tough plant. Use it in small pots that tend to dry out quickly because not much else will survive in tiny pots.

Growing

Lilyturf grows best in **light shade** or **partial shade** but tolerates both full sun and full shade well. The potting mix should be **humus rich, acidic, moist** and **well drained**. Fertilize monthly during the growing season with quarter-strength fertilizer. Where they are not hardy, plants will have to be stored in a shed or garage in winter or treated like annuals and replaced in spring.

Tips

Lilyturf is a good choice as a container groundcover in warm coastal gardens. If you have containers of shrubs and trees that you don't want to replant with annuals every year, lilyturf will form a low, dense mat of narrow, arching foliage with spikes of blue, purple or white flowers. It also makes an attractive addition to a mixed container.

Recommended

L. muscari forms low clumps of strap-like, evergreen leaves. It bears spikes of purple flowers from late summer on. **'Big Blue'** bears large spikes of purple-blue flowers. **'Monroe White'** has white flowers. **'Pee Dee Gold Ingot'** has golden yellow to chartreuse leaves that mature to bright yellow. It bears light purple flowers. **'Variegata'** has green-and-white-striped leaves and purple flowers.

Features: clump-forming, evergreen perennial; narrow, grass-like, dark green foliage; spikes of blue, purple or white, fall flowers **Height:** 8–18" **Spread:** 18"
Hardiness: zones 6–10

Lobelia
Lobelia

L. *erinus* cultivars and others (above)
L. *erinus* (below)

Both the annual and perennial selections of lobelia are interesting to use in container gardens. Each adds a unique touch.

Growing

All lobelias grow well in **full sun** or **partial shade**, with partial or light shade preferable for annual lobelia in hot and humid areas. The potting mix should be **humus rich, moist** and **well drained**. Fertilize every two to four weeks during the growing season with quarter-strength fertilizer. Cardinal flower tolerates wet soil. Cardinal flower should be moved to a sheltered location, preferably an unheated garage, in winter.

Features: bushy to upright habit; purple, blue, pink, white or red, summer to fall flowers   **Height:** 4–24"   **Spread:** 6" or more   **Hardiness:** zones 4–8; annual

Tips

Use annual lobelia in mixed containers or hanging baskets. The delicate, airy appearance adds a glaze of color that looks particularly attractive with broad-leaved plants such as hosta and lady's mantle.

Cardinal flower has a more upright habit, and its often bronzy foliage gives mixed containers an elegant appearance. Its ability to grow in moist to wet soil makes it suitable for boggy containers with other moisture lovers.

Recommended

L. cardinalis (cardinal flower) is a perennial that forms an upright clump of bronzy green foliage. It bears spikes of bright red flowers in summer and fall.

L. erinus (annual lobelia) may be rounded and bushy or low and trailing. It bears flowers in shades of blue, purple, red, pink or white. **Laguna Series** has heat-resistant, trailing plants with flowers in a variety of colors. **Riviera Series** has flowers in shades of blue and purple on compact, bushy plants.

L. x *speciosa* (hybrid cardinal flower) is a vigorous, bushy perennial. Hardiness varies from hybrid to hybrid. It bears flowers in shades of red, blue, purple, pink or white in summer and fall.

Trim annual lobelia back after the first wave of flowers. It will stop blooming in the hottest part of summer but usually revives in fall.

L. erinus 'Sapphire' with lamium and impatiens (above)
L. cardinalis (below)

Lotus Vine
Lotus

L. berthelotii with pansies

Lotus vine is also known as parrot's beak, coral gem and pelican's beak, names that make reference to the flowers' appearance.

Features: bushy or trailing habit; orange, red or yellow, summer through fall flowers
Height: 6–8"   **Spread:** 36" or more
Hardiness: tender perennial grown as an annual

Don't plant lotus vine solely for the flowers; this annual is highly sought after for its unique, ferny foliage and bushy but trailing growth habit. In the cool summer weather west of the Cascades, lotus vine may not bloom at all. The beautiful foliage will be the show instead.

Growing

Lotus vine grows well in **full sun** or **partial shade**. The potting mix should be **well drained**. This annual can tolerate hot and dry locations. Pinch the new tips back in late spring or early summer to promote bushier growth. Fertilize monthly with quarter-strength fertilizer.

Tips

Lotus vine is most effective when its striking, unique foliage is allowed to cascade over the side of a decorative pot, window box or planter. The flowers are bright and colorful, and they contrast with the silvery green, ferny foliage. Lotus vine complements purple- and yellow-flowering annuals and chartreuse- or bronze-leaved foliage plants very nicely.

Recommended

L. berthelotii is a trailing plant with silvery stems covered in fine, soft, needle-like foliage. Small clusters of vivid orange to scarlet flowers that resemble lobster claws are borne in spring and summer.

L. hirsutus is a bushy or trailing perennial with fine, gray-green foliage. It bears pink-flushed, white flowers in summer and fall.

L. x **'Amazon Sunset'** has gray-green, needle-like foliage and vibrantly hued yellow-orange flowers that darken toward the edge.

Lungwort
Pulmonaria

P. GAELIC SUNSET with impatiens and wishbone flower

The wide array of lungworts have highly attractive foliage that ranges in color from apple green to silver-spotted and olive to dark emerald green.

Growing

Lungworts prefer **partial to full shade**. The potting mix should be **humus rich, moist** and **well drained**. Mix in compost or earthworm castings. Fertilize monthly during the growing season with half-strength fertilizer. Move plants to a sheltered location in winter. Deadhead to keep plants tidy by removing the flower stems after flowering is finished. Cut the leaves right to the ground if they show signs of mildew or otherwise look ugly. Fresh, attractive growth will appear.

Tips

Lungworts are useful, attractive plants for shady and woodland-themed containers.

Their interesting foliage complements and contrasts brightly colored flowers.

Recommended

P. longifolia (long-leaved lungwort) forms a dense clump of long, narrow, white-spotted, green leaves and bears clusters of blue flowers. Cultivars are available.

P. officinalis (common lungwort) forms a loose clump of white-spotted, evergreen foliage. The flowers open pink and mature to blue. Cultivars are available.

P. saccharata (Bethlehem sage) forms a compact clump of large, white-spotted, evergreen leaves and purple, red or white flowers. Many cultivars and hybrids with other lungwort species are available.

Features: clump-forming perennial; decorative, mottled foliage; blue, red, pink or white, spring flowers **Height:** 8–24" **Spread:** 8–24" **Hardiness:** zones 3–8

Lysimachia
Lysimachia

L. nummularia with blue fescue, snapdragon, fan flower and lamium

Not to be confused with purple loosestrife (Lythrum salicaria), which has been banned because of its invasive nature in wetlands, true loosestrife works well just about anywhere in the garden.

These vigorous, carefree plants will enjoy a spot in a moist bog-themed container planting.

Growing
Lysimachia grows well in **full sun** or **partial shade**. The potting mix should be **moist** and **well drained**, though this plant is tolerant of wet soil. Fertilize monthly during the growing season with quarter- to half-strength fertlizer. Move containers to a sheltered location protected from temperature fluctuations in winter.

Tips
The low, spreading creeping Jenny will form a dense mat that spills over the edges of your containers and creeps into any others you have positioned close by. The contrasting foliage of golden creeping Jenny works well planted with lungwort or blue-leaved hosta. Gooseneck loosestrife is a good upright companion plant for a mixed container.

Recommended
L. clethroides (gooseneck loosestrife) is a bushy, upright plant with deep green foliage that turns brilliant bronzy red in fall. Tall spikes of white flowers, bent like a goose's neck, are borne on purple stems in mid- and late summer.

L. nummularia (creeping Jenny) is a prostrate, spreading plant with trailing stems. It bears bright yellow flowers on and off all summer. **'Goldilocks'** (golden creeping Jenny) produces golden foliage with yellow flowers.

Also called: loosestrife **Features:** yellow or white flowers in spring and summer
Height: 2–36" **Spread:** 18–36"
Hardiness: zones 2–8

Maidenhair Fern

Adiantum

These charming and delicate-looking ferns add a graceful touch to any shady container planting. Their unique habit and texture will stand out in any combination.

Growing

Maidenhair fern grows well in **light to partial shade** but tolerates full shade. The potting mix should be **humus rich, slightly acidic** and **moist**. Fertilize monthly during the growing season with quarter-strength fertilizer. Move northern maidenhair fern to a sheltered location in winter. Bring giant maidenhair fern indoors and keep it in a cool, bright room in winter.

Tips

These lovely ferns will do well in any shaded spot. Include them in mixed containers, where they make beautiful, arching companions to other shade-lovers such as hosta, lungwort and coral bells. They also look nice with colorful flowers.

Recommended

A. formosum (giant maidenhair fern) is a tender species that is sometimes grown as a houseplant. It has stunning, arching fronds that give the whole plant a cascading appearance. It is worth searching for and including in a mixed container, where it is sure to be an elegant beauty.

A. pedatum (northern maidenhair fern) is a hardy perennial that forms a spreading mound of delicate, arching fronds arranged in a horseshoe or circular pattern. Its light green leaflets stand out against the black stems and turn bright yellow in fall. These ferns look especially attractive in shiny, black ceramic or painted metal pots. The pot will color echo the dark stems.

A. pedatum with dracaena, oxalis and coleus

These fine-textured plants give mixed containers a light, airy appearance.

Features: deciduous fern; summer and fall foliage; habit **Height:** 12–36" **Spread:** 12–24" **Hardiness:** zones 3–8; tender perennial grown as an annual

Maple
Acer

A. *ginnala* 'Bailey Compact'

Maple fruits, called samaras, have wings that act like miniature helicopter rotors and help in seed dispersal.

Features: small, multi-stemmed, deciduous tree or large shrub; colorful or decorative foliage that turns stunning shades of red, yellow or orange in fall   **Height:** 2–15'
Spread: 2–15'   **Hardiness:** zones 2–8

aples are attractive all year long, boasting delicate flowers in spring, attractive foliage and hanging samaras in summer, vibrant leaf color in fall and interesting bark and branch structures in winter.

Growing
Maples do well in **full sun** or **light shade**. The potting mix should be **humus rich** and **well drained**. Fertilize no more than monthly during the growing season with quarter-strength

fertilizer. Tender maples should be
moved into a shed or garage in winter.
Hardy maples will do fine in a spot protected from temperature fluctuations.

Tips

Maples can be used as specimen trees
in containers on patios or terraces. A
Japanese-style garden can be created in
containers with a maple or two to add
height and volume. Almost all maples
can be used to create bonsai specimens.

Recommended

A. ginnala (amur maple) is an extremely
hardy, rounded to spreading tree that
has attractive, dark green leaves, bright
red samaras and smooth bark with dis-
tinctive vertical striping. The fall foliage
is often a brilliant crimson. The color
develops best in full sun, but the tree
will also grow well in light shade.

A. griseum (paperbark maple) is a
rounded to oval tree with exfoliating,
orange-brown bark that peels and curls
away from the trunk in papery strips.
The foliage turns red, orange or yellow
in fall. (Zones 4–8)

A. japonicum (fullmoon maple,
Japanese maple) is an open, spreading
tree or large shrub. The leaves turn
stunning shades of yellow, orange
or red in fall. (Zones 5–7)

A. palmatum (Japanese maple) is
a rounded, spreading or cascading,
small tree that develops red, yellow or
orange fall color. Two distinct groups
of cultivars have been developed. Types
without dissected leaves, derived from
A. p. var. *atropurpureum,* are grown
for their purple foliage. Types with
dissected leaves, derived from *A. p.* var.
dissectum, have foliage so deeply lobed
and divided that it appears fern-like
or even thread-like. The leaves can be
green, red or purple. (Zones 6–8)

A. palmatum 'Bloodgood' (above)

A. japonicum (center), *A. griseum* (below)

Million Bells

Calibrachoa

C. Superbells Series 'Trailing Blue'

Million bells are charming plants that will bloom continuously throughout the growing season.

Growing

Million bells prefer to grow in **full sun**. The potting mix should be **moist** and **well drained**. Fertilize every two weeks with half-strength fertilizer. Although they prefer to be watered regularly, million bells are fairly drought resistant in cool and warm climates. Million bells will bloom well into fall.

Tips

Million bells are deservedly popular for planters and hanging baskets. They can stand alone, filling and trailing over the edge of just about any container, and also make lovely additions to mixed containers, where the colorful flowers will stand out against a background of any shade of green, bronze or chartreuse.

Recommended

C. **hybrids** have a dense, trailing habit. They all bear small, yellow-centered flowers that resemble petunias. There are many cultivars available, and more beautiful plants with a wider range of flower colors become available each year. Two main series for these plants are **Million Bells Series** and **Superbells Series**. Both offer plants with flowers in shades of blue, pink, red, yellow, orange or white. Several bicolored options are also available, including yellow-orange, mottled and pink-veined white.

Also called: calibrachoa   **Features:** trailing habit; pink, purple, blue, red, yellow, orange, white or bicolored flowers   **Height:** 6–12"   **Spread:** 24"   **Hardiness:** tender perennial grown as an annual

Mondo Grass

Ophiopogon

Mondo grass is an excellent accent and contrast plant. The foliage makes a stunning background to highlight any brightly colored plant or flower.

Growing

Mondo grass grows best in **full sun to light shade**. The potting mix should be **humus rich, moist** and **well drained**. Fertilize monthly during the growing season with quarter- to half-strength fertilizer. Treat these plants like annuals or move containers to an unheated garage or shed in winter to protect them from temperature fluctuations.

Tips

Use this short, grassy perennial in front of other grasses and accent it with a collection of river stones or glass pebbles. It will have a calming effect when used by itself in a pot. The foliage contrasts nicely with many colorful plants.

Recommended

O. japonicus (mondo grass, monkey grass) produces an evergreen mat of lush, dark green, grass-like foliage. Short spikes of white, occasionally lilac-tinged flowers emerge in summer, followed by metallic blue fruit. Many cultivars are available. Plants are hardy to zone 6 with protection.

O. planiscapus 'Ebknizam' (EBONY NIGHT) has curving, almost black leaves and dark lavender flowers. NIGRA (black mondo grass, black lily turf), a Proven Selection by Proven Winners, is a clumping, spreading plant with dark purple, almost black leaves and pink to mauve flowers.

O. planiscapus NIGRA

This plant is not a grass at all—it is a member of the lily family.

Features: low, clump-forming habit; uniquely colored foliage; lavender, pink or white flowers
Height: 4–12"   **Spread:** 6–12"
Hardiness: zones 5–9; perennial grown as an annual

Monkey Flower
Mimulus

M. x hybridus 'Mystic'

The markings on the face of the flowers look like monkey faces to some people.

Features: bushy, upright or trailing habit; flowers in bright and pastel shades of orange, yellow, burgundy, pink, red, cream or bicolors
Height: 6–12"   **Spread:** 12–24"
Hardiness: zones 6–9; semi-hardy perennial grown as an annual

The name alone makes these good plants for a tropical-themed container garden. A wide range of colors and a floriferous habit are bonuses.

Growing
Monkey flowers prefer **light shade** or **partial shade** with protection from the afternoon sun. The potting mix should be **humus rich** and **moist to wet**. Mix in compost or earthworm castings. Fertilize every two weeks in summer with quarter- to half-strength fertilizer. Plants can be brought indoors at the end of summer and grown as houseplants in a cool, bright room until spring.

Tips
Monkey flowers make an excellent addition to a bog-themed mixed container because they naturally grow alongside streams. Many of the other moisture-loving plants are foliage plants or flower for only a short time, so these colorful bloomers are a welcome addition.

Recommended
M. aurantiacus is an upright to relaxed plant with glossy, sticky, bright green leaves. It bears dark red, orange or yellow flowers in late summer.

M. x hybridus is a group of upright plants with spotted flowers. **'Calypso Mixed'** has flowers in a wide range of colors. **Mystic Series** are compact and early-flowering plants that offer a wide range of bright flower colors in solids or bicolors.

M. luteus (yellow monkey flower) has a spreading habit and attractive, yellow flowers sometimes spotted with red or purple.

Nasturtium
Tropaeolum

T. majus 'Jewel'

There is almost nothing as lovely as the wonderful red, orange or yellow flowers dotting a planting of nasturtiums as they tumble over the edges of a tall terra-cotta pot.

Growing

Nasturtiums prefer **full sun** but tolerate some shade. The potting mix should be **light, moist** and **well drained**. Too much fertilizer will result in lots of leaves and very few flowers, so fertilize no more than monthly with quarter-strength fertilizer. Let the soil drain completely between waterings.

Tips

Nasturtiums are used in containers and hanging baskets. The climbing varieties can be grown up trellises or left to spill over the edge of a container and ramble around. The bushy selections can be used in mixed containers with other red-, yellow- or orange-flowered plants, or with other edible-flowered plants like pansies for a themed container.

Recommended

T. majus is a bushy plant or a trailing or climbing plant. It bears bright red, yellow or orange flowers all summer. The bright green leaves are round with wavy margins. 'Alaska' has cream-mottled foliage and a bushy habit. 'Jewel' has bushy plants with flowers in shades of red, scarlet, pink, yellow, cream or orange, some with darker-veined throats.

Features: trailing, climbing or bushy habit; bright red, orange, yellow, scarlet, pink, cream, gold, white or bicolored flowers; attractive, round, sometimes variegated foliage; edible leaves and flowers   **Height:** 12–18" for dwarf varieties; up to 10' for trailing varieties   **Spread:** equal to height   **Hardiness:** annual

Nemesia
Nemesia

N. SUNSATIA PINEAPPLE and others

Nemesias make a bright and color-ful addition to the front of a mixed container planting.

Growing

Nemesias grow best in **full sun**. The potting mix should be **slightly acidic, moist** and **well drained**. Regular watering will keep these plants blooming through summer. Fertilize every two weeks with quarter-strength fertilizer when plants are actively growing and blooming. Nemesias ben-efit from being cut back hard when the flowering cycle slows down.

Features: bushy, mound-forming habit; red, blue, purple, pink, white, yellow, orange or bicolored flowers **Height:** 6–24"
Spread: 4–12" **Hardiness:** tender perennial grown as an annual

Tips

Nemesias are beautiful little plants that are best used in mixed containers because they tend to stop blooming during the hottest part of summer.

Recommended

N. hybrids are bushy and mound forming or trailing and have bright green foliage. They bear flowers in shades of blue, purple, white, pink, red or yellow, often in bicolors. **'Bluebird'** bears lavender blue flowers on low, bushy plants. **Carnival Series** plants are compact and bear many flowers in yellow, white, orange, pink or red. **'KLM'** has bicolored blue and white flowers with yellow throats. Proven Winners Selection SUNSATIA SERIES includes colorful cultivars that may be bushy or trailing and several that are heat resistant.

Nicotiana
Nicotiana

These bushy, sticky plants topped with clusters of tubular flowers attract night-flying pollinators such as moths.

Growing

Nicotiana will grow equally well in **full sun**, **light shade** or **partial shade**. The potting mix should be **humus rich, moist** and **well drained**. Fertilize every two weeks with half-strength fertilizer.

Tips

The dwarf selections seem best suited for small mixed containers, but the taller selections make excellent center plants with low, bushy and trailing plants surrounding their feet.

Recommended

N. alata is an upright plant that has a strong, sweet fragrance. **Merlin Series** has dwarf plants with red, pink, purple, white or pale green flowers. **Nicki Series** has compact or dwarf plants with fragrant blooms in many colors.

N. **'Lime Green'** is an upright plant that bears clusters of lime green flowers.

N. sylvestris is a tall, upright plant that bears white blooms that are fragrant in the evening.

Nicotiana was originally cultivated for the wonderful scent of its flowers. At first, the flowers were only green and opened only in the evening and at night. In attempts to expand the variety of colors and have the flowers open during the day, the popular scent has, in some cases, been lost.

N. alata Nicki Series and *N. sylvestris* with cleome

Features: sticky, rosette-forming to bushy, upright habit; red, pink, green, yellow, white or purple, sometimes fragrant flowers **Height:** 1–5' **Spread:** 12" **Hardiness:** annual

Oregano
Origanum

O. vulgare var. *hirtum* 'Aureum' with marigold, parsley and tarragon

Oregano is a lovely, fragrant plant with a compact, rounded habit and decorative foliage.

Growing

Oregano grows best in **full sun**. The potting mix should be **neutral to alkaline** and **well drained**. Fertilize no more than once a month during the growing season with quarter-strength fertilizer. In winter, move hardy plants to a sheltered location; where they are not hardy, move them to an unheated shed or garage.

Tips

Try growing several different oreganos in individual containers of different heights to create a grouping, or plant different herbs in each pot for a more varied display.

Recommended

O. laevigatum is a shrubby, upright perennial that bears rosy purple flowers. **'Hopley's Purple'** bears dark purple flowers and is hardy to zone 6.

O. vulgare subsp. *hirtum* (oregano, Greek oregano) is a low-growing, bushy plant with hairy, gray-green leaves and white flowers. **'Aureum'** has bright golden leaves and pink flowers. **'Aureum Crispum'** has a spreading habit and curly, golden leaves. **'Zorba Red'** has a spreading habit with bright red-purple bracts and white flowers. **'Zorba White'** has greenish bracts and white flowers.

Features: bushy perennial; fragrant, sometimes colorful foliage; white or pink, summer flowers **Height:** 10–24" **Spread:** 8–12" **Hardiness:** zones 5–9

In Greek, oros *means "mountain" and* ganos *means "joy" or "beauty," so oregano translates as "joy" or "beauty of the mountain."*

Oxalis

Oxalis

Oxalis readily fills little spaces with dense, lustrous foliage and teeny, tiny flowers that never cease to amaze.

Growing

Oxalis prefers **full sun** or **partial shade** but tolerates full shade with reduced flowering. The potting mix should be **humus rich** and **well drained**. Fertilize every two weeks with quarter-strength fertilizer.

Tips

Oxalis is becoming increasingly popular for container culture, with new varieties appearing annually. Oxalis works well mixed with other plants and is equally stunning all by itself.

Recommended

O. crassipes is a vigorous, mound-forming species with bright green leaves and lemon yellow flowers. **'Alba'** bears green leaves and tiny, white flowers. It is tolerant of extreme heat and drought. **'Rosea'** has pink flowers.

O. regnellii is a vigorous, shade-loving species. It produces large, shamrock-shaped foliage and dainty flowers. Watch for the CHARMED SERIES from Proven Winners.

O. vulcanicola is a small, bushy, spreading plant with reddish stems, green foliage flushed with red, and yellow flowers with purple-red veining. **'Copper Tones'** and **'Molten Lava'** have gold foliage with a touch of rust and buttery yellow flowers at the tips of reddish stems. **'Zinfandel,'** a Proven Selection by Proven Winners, produces dark burgundy, almost black foliage and tiny, vivid yellow blooms.

O. vulcanicola 'Zinfandel' and others

Tiny, decorative pots of O. crassipes *are often found in garden centers and gift shops around St. Patrick's Day.*

Features: bushy or spreading habit; colorful foliage; yellow, white or pink flowers
Height: 6–12"   **Spread:** 6–12" or more
Hardiness: tender perennial grown as an annual

Pansy
Viola

V. x wittrockiana cultivar with vinca, coral bells and dracaena

Colorful and cheerful, pansy flowers are a welcome sight in spring after a long, dreary winter.

Johnny-jump-ups self-seed prolifically and may turn up from year to year in not only the container they were growing in, but in other containers too.

Features: blue, purple, red, orange, yellow, pink or white, bicolored or multi-colored flowers **Height:** 3–10" **Spread:** 6–12" **Hardiness:** zones 5–9; often grown as an annual

Growing

Pansies prefer **full sun** but tolerate partial shade. The potting mix should be **moist** and **well drained**. Fertilize every two weeks during the growing season with quarter-strength fertilizer. Pansies do best when the weather is cool and often die back completely in summer. Plants may rejuvenate in fall, but it is often easier to plant new ones. Deadhead to keep these plants blooming and to prevent self-seeding.

Tips

Pansies make good companions for spring-flowering bulbs and primroses. A pot of spring pansies set where you can see it from indoors will remind you that summer is just around the corner. For a dramatic spring display, use pansies around the base of potted tulips and daffodils.

Recommended

V. cornuta (horned violet, viola) is a low-growing, spreading plant. The flowers are usually in shades of blue, purple or white. **Chalon Hybrids** bear ruffled, bicolored or multi-colored flowers in shades of blue, red, rose or white. **Sorbet Series** has a wide color range. Planted in fall, they flower until the ground freezes and may surprise you with another show in spring. '**Sorbet Yesterday, Today and Tomorrow**' bears flowers that open white and gradually turn purple as they mature.

V. tricolor (Johnny-jump-up) is a popular species. The flowers are purple, white and yellow, usually in combination, although several varieties have flowers in a single color, often purple.

V. x wittrockiana (pansy) comes in blue, purple, red, orange, yellow, pink or white, often multi-colored or with face-like markings. '**Antique Shades Mix**' offers pastel combinations of plum, yellow, apricot, rust and cream. '**Can Can Mix**' bears frilly flowers with ruffled edges in bicolored and multi-colored combinations of yellow, purple, red, white, pink and blue. **Imperial Series** includes plants that bear large flowers in a range of unique colors. '**Imperial Frosty Rose**' has flowers with deep rose pink centers that gradually pale to white near the edges of the petals.

V. x wittrockiana cultivar with calla lily (above)
V. x wittrockiana (below)

Parsley
Petroselinum

P. *crispum* with others

Parsley leaves make a tasty and nutritious addition to salads. Tear freshly picked leaves and sprinkle them over your mixed greens.

The tightly curled leaves and bright green color of parsley provide an unmatched display to fill in the spaces among the other plants in your containers.

Growing
Parsley grows well in **full sun** or **partial shade**. The potting mix should be **humus rich, moist** and **well drained**. Fertilize every two weeks with quarter-strength fertilizer. Direct sow seeds because the plants resent transplanting. The seeds can take several weeks to sprout. Soak the seeds in warm water for 24 hours before sowing to speed up germination.

Tips
Containers of parsley can be kept close to the house for easy picking if you are growing it for eating or garnish—you could have several pots containing different herbs. Parsley is also a fantastic mixer plant for containers. Its bushy growth fills in quickly, and the bright green creates a good background for bright red, scarlet or orange flowers in particular.

Recommended
P. crispum forms a clump of bright green, divided leaves. This plant is a biennial but is usually grown as an annual because it is the leaves that are desired, not the flowers or seeds. Cultivars may have flat or curly leaves. Flat leaves are more flavorful and curly are more decorative. Dwarf cultivars are also available.

Features: clump-forming habit; attractive foliage   **Height:** 8–24"   **Spread:** 12–24"
Hardiness: zones 5–8; biennial grown as an annual

Penstemon

Penstemon

P. LILLIPUT ROSE, a Proven Winners Selection, with nemesia and coleus

Mix one or two penstemons into your containers, and they will be sure to attract hummingbirds to your garden.

Growing

Penstemons prefer **full sun** but tolerate partial shade. The potting mix should be **very well drained**. Add one-third sand or perlite to the potting mix to ensure quick drainage. These plants are quite drought tolerant. Fertilize once at the beginning of the growing season at half the normal rate with slow-release fertilizer. Move containers to a sheltered location protected from temperature fluctuations in winter.

Tips

These plants tend to be tall and slender and are prone to falling over unless surrounded by supportive neighbors. Growing *Sedum* 'Autumn Joy' in front of penstemons will help keep them upright. They are ideal for mixed containers.

Recommended

P. barbatus (beardlip penstemon) is an upright, rounded perennial. Red or pink flowers are borne from early summer to early fall. **'Hyacinth Mix'** is a mix of pink, lilac, blue and scarlet.

P. digitalis **'Husker Red'** is an upright, semi-evergreen that has red stems and red-purple new foliage. It bears white flowers veined with red all summer.

P. fruticosus **'Purple Haze'** is a mound-forming, evergreen subshrub. It bears purple flowers prolifically in late spring. When placed near a wall edge or overhang, it will trail over the edge.

Also called: beard-tongue **Features:** white, yellow, pink, purple or red, spring, summer or fall flowers **Height:** 18"–5' **Spread:** 12–24" **Hardiness:** zones 4–9

Perilla
Perilla

P. 'Magellanica,' a Proven Selections plant from Proven Winners, and others

Growing

Perilla prefers **full sun** or **partial shade**. The potting mix should be **fertile, moist** and **well drained**. Soil amended with compost or well-composted manure is of added benefit. Plants can be pinched for more bushiness. Perilla may self-seed prolifically.

Tips

Perilla is the perfect alternative to coleus and is an ideal complement to brightly colored annuals and perennials in decorative containers. Use a deep bronze perilla in the center of a terra-cotta pot and surround it with bright orange and yellow marigolds for a strong combination that can handle the heat.

Recommended

P. frutescens is a vigorous annual with deeply toothed, medium green, purple-flecked, cinnamon-lemon flavored leaves. Tiny, white flowers are borne on spikes in summer, but this annual is grown more for its ornate, colorful foliage. **'Atropurpurea'** (beefsteak plant) bears dark purple-red leaves. **Var. crispa** (var. *nankinensis*; 'Crispa') has dark bronze to purple foliage with very frilly leaf margins. **'Magilla'** ('Magilla Purple') bears multi-colored leaves of purple, green, white and pink, and **'Magilla Vanilla'** bears white and green leaves.

*P*erilla is well known for its tolerance of summer heat and will easily compete with some of the most aggressive summer annuals. Recently, breeders have introduced more decorative selections to the market, making perilla highly sought after.

Also called: shiso, Chinese basil
Features: bushy, vigorous habit; ornate, colorful foliage   **Height:** 12–24"
Spread: 12–24"   **Hardiness:** annual

Petunia
Petunia

P. x *hybrida* with English ivy and reed palm

For speedy growth, prolific blooming, ease of care and a huge number of varieties, petunias are hard to beat. The rekindling of interest in petunias resulted largely from the development of many exciting new varieties.

Growing

Petunias prefer **full sun**. The potting mix should be **well drained**. Fertilize

Petunias can be enjoyed as cut flowers. Regular cutting of blooms helps keep the plants bushy. The purple and white petunias tend to be the most fragrant.

Features: bushy to trailing habit; summer flowers in shades of pink, blue, purple, red, coral, yellow or white, or bicolored
Height: 6–18"   **Spread:** 12–24" or wider
Hardiness: annual

P. milliflora (above), Lavender Wave (below)

Tips

Use petunias in containers and hanging baskets. Planted alone, their bushy growth will fill a container and spill over the edge. The rich colors of their flowers also make them excellent companions for other annuals as well as for any container plantings of shrubs or small trees.

Recommended

P. x *hybrida* is a large group of popular, sun-loving annuals that fall into three categories: grandifloras, with the largest flowers; multifloras, bearing many medium-sized flowers; and millifloras, with the smallest flowers. In western Washington and Oregon, choose the millifloras because they do best in wet weather.

P. **Storm Series** are grandiflora petunias that are weather and disease tolerant and bear large blooms in a range of colors.

P. **Supertunia Series** offers flowers in a wide range of pinks and purples, but there are also red, white and yellow selections.

P. **Wave Series** are vigorous, low-growing, spreading plants that bloom almost non-stop in a range of colors. They are tolerant of rain and cold. Look for **'Blue,' 'Pink,' 'Purple,' 'Misty Lilac,' 'Lavender'** and **'Rose.' Tidal Wave Series** are upright, spreading plants. Selections include **'Cherry,' 'Pink Hot,' 'Purple'** and **'Silver.' Easy Wave Series** are mound-forming petunias similar to the original Wave Series, but a little taller. Easy Wave selections include **'Blue,' 'Coral Reef,' 'Mystic Pink,' 'Pink,' 'Red,' 'Rosy Dawn,' 'Salmon,' 'Shell Pink'** and **'White.'**

no more than monthly with quarter-strength fertilizer. Pinch halfway back in mid-summer to keep plants bushy and to encourage new growth and flowers.

Phormium

Phormium

The bronze-leaved phormiums are the most hardy. They will overwinter outdoors near the coast if the pots are placed where they will be protected from too much rain.

Growing

Phormiums grow best in **full sun** but appreciate some protection from the hot afternoon sun. The potting mix should be **moist** and **well drained**. Fertilize every two weeks during the growing season with half-strength fertilizer. Plants grown in containers can be overwintered in a bright, cool, frost-free location indoors.

Tips

Use phormiums in container plantings near entryways and walkways. Their bold and exotic foliage will draw the eye and encourage visitors to come closer for a better look. Mix brightly colored coleus with phormium, and you'll have a pot bursting with tropical delight.

Recommended

P. **'Sundowner'** forms a clump of broad, upright foliage. The light, bronzy green foliage is margined with pink and yellow. This variety will not overwinter outdoors.

P. tenax (New Zealand flax) forms a large clump of long, stiff, dark green leaves with gray-green undersides. **'Aurora'** has bronzy green leaves striped with pink, yellow and red. **'Veitchianum'** has cream-striped, green leaves.

P. **'Yellow Wave'** forms a clump of yellow-green leaves striped with darker green.

Large, loose, spikes of small flowers are sometimes produced in summer.

P. tenax cultivar with echivaria and hens and chicks

Also called: New Zealand flax   **Features:** clump-forming habit; green, black, red or yellow, often multi-colored and striped foliage **Height:** 2–8'   **Spread:** 2–8'   **Hardiness:** zones 9–10; tender perennial grown as an annual

Piggyback Plant
Tolmiea

T. menziesii

iggyback plant uniquely produces new plantlets from the surface of an existing leaf, hence the common name.

Growing
Piggyback plant grows best in **full shade, light shade** or **partial shade** with protection from the hot afternoon sun. The potting mix should be **moist** and **well drained**. Fertilize monthly during the growing season with quarter-strength fertilizer. Spray the leaves often with a strong jet of water to keep them free of spider mites, which can be a problem during warm weather. Winter plants in a cool, bright room where they are

Also called: thousand mothers, youth-on-age **Features:** clump-forming habit; decorative, piggyback foliage **Height:** 12–18" **Spread:** 12–18" **Hardiness:** zones 6–9; perennial grown as an annual

not hardy. Where they are hardy, move plants to a sheltered location protected from temperature fluctuations.

Tips
Piggyback plant is often grown in hanging baskets. The mounded leaves are weighted down by newly produced foliage, creating a cascading appearance. This plant is an ideal addition to an understory-themed container or for a container on a heavily shaded balcony.

Recommended
T. menziesii is a clump-forming plant with hairy, heart-shaped leaves with toothed edges. Small plantlets emerge where the leaf and stem join. Tiny, tubular, greenish, insignificant flowers open along one side of the leaf. **'Variegata'** has yellow-splashed leaves, and **'Taff's Gold'** produces both solid and variegated leaves.

Plectranthus
Plectranthus

These mound-forming plants, with their often aromatic foliage, eventually develop a more trailing habit. They are related to coleus and are native to tropical climates.

Growing

Plectranthus grows best in **light shade** or **partial shade**. The potting mix should be **moist** and **well drained**. Fertilize every two weeks with quarter- to half-strength fertilizer.

Tips

These trailing plants make fabulous fillers for hanging baskets and mixed containers. Place them near a walkway or other area where people will be able to brush past the plants and smell the spicy-scented foliage. Pair them with bananas or canna lilies to add a jungle look to large container gardens.

Recommended

P. argentatus is an upright to spreading plant with silvery green, hairy stems and leaves. It bears clusters of small, bluish white flowers near the ends of stems, in summer. It can grow in full sun in western Washington and Oregon, but morning sun only in the hotter eastern parts.

P. ciliatus is a low-growing, trailing plant with burgundy stems and lilac blue flowers. The dark to olive green, toothed foliage has burgundy undersides. **'Vanilla Twist'** has bright green leaves with white, scalloped margins.

P. forsteri is a mounding then trailing plant with light green, slightly hairy leaves and clusters of small, white or pale purple flowers in summer. **'Marginatus'** has cream-edged leaves.

P. ciliatus 'Vanilla Twist,' a Proven Winners Selection, with sedge, purple fountain grass, English ivy and coleus

The trailing stems root easily from cuttings; start some in late summer to grow indoors through winter.

Features: bushy to trailing habit; decorative foliage **Height:** 8–12" **Spread:** about 36" **Hardiness:** annual; tender perennial grown as an annual

Poor Man's Orchid
Schizanthus

S. pinnatus cultivar

These plants have a short flowering season when grown east of the Cascades or in hot summer climates. You can replace them with mums halfway through summer.

Features: pink, red, yellow or purple, usually bicolored flowers whose yellow throats are marked with contrasting streaks and blotches
Height: 6–24"   **Spread:** 9–12"
Hardiness: annual

The most spectacular hanging baskets I've ever admired can be seen each June hanging from the lightposts in Victoria, B.C. Poor man's orchids flow over the edges of these baskets and bloom happily in a cocktail of flower shapes and forms.

Growing
Poor man's orchid grows best in **full sun to partial shade** but appreciates some relief from the hot afternoon sun. This plant does not tolerate frost or excess heat and also does quite well planted in light shade. The soil should be **fertile, moist** and **well drained**.

Tips
Poor man's orchid can be used in hanging baskets and mixed containers. It does best in cool summer climates. This plant combines well with most other annuals.

Recommended
S. **'Angel Wings'** is a trailing hybrid bearing flowers ranging from pale pink to lavender to deep violet.

S. pinnatus is an erect plant with light green, fern-like leaves. **'Dwarf Bouquet Mixed'** are short, compact plants, growing to 16", and are good container plants. The flowers are shades of red, orange, pink and orange-yellow. **'Royal Pierrot Mixed'** have rich colors in pink, purple, purple-blue and white. **'Star Parade'** is a compact variety available in several colors. It grows up to 10" tall.

Purple Fountain Grass
Pennisetum

P. setaceum BURGUNDY GIANT with euphorbia, mondo grass, coleus, English ivy and dwarf plumbago

urple fountain grass has a graceful, soft but also bold form that makes it a stunning companion in a mixed container.

Growing

Purple fountain grass grows best in **full sun**. The potting mix should be **well drained**. Fertilize monthly during the growing season with quarter-strength fertilizer. Where hardy, purple fountain grass should be overwintered in a

Choose a sleek metal or shiny contemporary pot for this decorative grass and mulch the soil with shiny, black, flat stones. You'll have a living piece of modern art for your patio or deck.

Features: arching or upright habit; decorative foliage; fuzzy, pink, purple or tan, summer and fall flowers   **Height:** 1–6'
Spread: 18"–4'   **Hardiness:** zones 5–10; tender perennial grown as an annual

P. setaceum 'Rubrum' (above)
P. glaucum 'Purple Majesty' with others (below)

sheltered location out of the wind and sun and protected from temperature fluctuations. Where not hardy, it can be cut back in fall and stored in a cool location indoors, or treated as an annual.

Tips

Purple fountain grass is an interesting, low-maintenance alternative to dracaena in mixed containers. The colorful foliage can be used to create color-themed containers with perennials and annuals, whether you complement or contrast the colors.

Recommended

P. alopecuriodes forms clumps of long, narrow, bright green, arching leaves. Soft spikes of tan, pink or purple, fuzzy flowers are produced on long, arching stems in summer and fall. **'Hameln'** is a dwarf cultivar hardy to zone 5. **'Little Bunny'** is an even smaller selection that grows only 12" tall. (Zones 6–9)

P. glaucum **'Purple Majesty'** (purple majesty millet, ornamental millet) has a corn-like growth habit, with a strong central stalk and broad, blackish purple, strap-like leaves. The bottlebrush-like flower spikes are also purple, though the tiny flowers may be yellow. (Zones 8–10)

P. setaceum **'Rubrum'** ('Purpureum,' annual fountain grass) is a dense, mound-forming, tender perennial grown as an annual. It has narrow, dark purple foliage and large, showy, rose-red flower spikes from mid-summer to fall. BURGUNDY GIANT, a Proven Selection by Proven Winners, has wider, deep burgundy foliage. Its nodding flower spikes are pinkish purple. (Zones 9–10)

Rhododendron · Azalea
Rhododendron

Pacific Northwest gardeners can say a word or two of heartfelt thanks that these beautiful shrubs, with their photogenic foliage and huge, abundant, colorful blossoms, grow so well for us.

Growing

Rhododendrons prefer **partial shade** or **light shade**, but they tolerate full sun if the container is kept moist. Provide shelter from strong winds. The potting mix should be **fertile, humus rich, acidic, moist** and **well drained**. Add one-third of the container volume of peat moss to the potting mix for the acidity and extra water-holding capacity. Feed in spring at full strength as soon as the container soil warms, then quarter- to half-strength fertilizer every four to six weeks until mid-July. Use fertilizer recommended for rhododendrons, but

---

Features: mounding to rounded, evergreen or deciduous shrub; late-winter to early-summer flowers; attractive foliage
Height: 2–12'   **Spread:** 2–12'
Hardiness: zones 3–9

don't overdo it; rhododendrons in pots are susceptible to fertilizer burn.

Mulch with bark chips to keep the shallow roots cool in summer. Remove dead and damaged growth in mid-spring. Spent flower clusters should be removed if possible. Grasp the base of the cluster between your thumb and forefinger and twist to remove the entire cluster. Be careful not to damage the new buds that form directly beneath the flowerheads.

Tips
These gorgeous shrubs are best used as specimen plants. They look great when underplanted with shade-tolerant ground-covers such as lamium and bugleweed.

Recommended
R. **Kurume Hybrids** are deciduous, dwarf azaleas that grow 24–36" tall and wide. The spring flowers bloom mostly in shades of red, pink and white, but shades of orange and purple are also available. (Zones 5–8)

R. **Northern Lights Hybrids** are broad, rounded, deciduous azaleas that grow about 5' tall and 4' wide. These cold-hardy hybrids are available with yellow-orange, yellow, light purple, dark pink, light orange-red or white flowers. (Zones 3–7)

R. **PJM Hybrids** are compact, rounded, dwarf, evergreen rhododendrons. They grow 3–6' tall with an equal spread. These hybrids are weevil resistant and have mostly pink or purple flowers. They are wind and cold resistant and survive the cold winters east of the Cascades better than the more tender rhododendrons. (Zones 4–8)

R. yakushimanum (Yakushima rhodo-dendron) is a dense, mounding, evergreen rhododendron that grows 36" tall and wide. Rose red buds open to reveal white flowers in mid-spring. The underside of the foliage is soft and fuzzy. (Zones 5–9)

Rose
Rosa

There are many roses that will thrive in containers, though most will eventually have to be moved to the garden.

Growing
Roses grow best in **full sun**. The potting mix should be **humus rich, slightly acidic, moist** and **well drained**. Fertilize every two weeks during the growing season with half-strength fertilizer. Deadhead lightly to keep plants tidy and to encourage prolific blooming, except Hansa and Knock Out, which develop attractive hips after the flowers are done.

Tips
Bushy modern shrub roses, miniature roses and hardy roses such as the

R. 'Knock Out' (above & below)

Features: rounded to arching shrub; often-fragrant, mid-summer to fall flowers
Height: 1–4'   **Spread:** 1–4'
Hardiness: zones 3–9

R. 'Hansa' (above), R. 'Cupcake' (below)

rugosas are the best choices for containers. The miniatures make good companions for mixed containers, while the larger, shrubbier roses make good focal points, perhaps with trailing, white-flowered plants such as bacopas planted around them.

Recommended

R. **'Cupcake'** is a compact, bushy miniature shrub rose with glossy, green foliage. It produces clusters of light to medium pink flowers all summer. It grows 12–18" tall, with an equal spread. (Zones 5–9)

R. **'George Vancouver'** is a hardy, mound-forming Explorer rose that maintains a neat, rounded habit. The medium red, double flowers may be borne singly or in clusters of up to six. It grows about 24" tall and wide.

R. **'Hansa'** is a hardy, arching rugosa rose with deeply veined, glossy, leathery foliage. The fragrant, mauve purple to mauve red, double flowers are followed by scarlet hips. It grows about 4' tall and wide.

R. **'Knock Out'** has an attractive, rounded form with glossy, green leaves that turn to shades of burgundy in fall. The bright, cherry red flowers are borne in clusters almost all summer and fall. Orange-red hips last well into winter. It grows about 4' tall and wide and is disease resistant. (Zones 4–9)

Miniature roses like Cupcake can be overwintered indoors in a cool, bright room.

Rosemary
Rosmarinus

These pretty little ever-greens have fragrant foliage and varied habits that make them worth growing in a container near your kitchen.

Growing

Rosemary prefers **full sun** but tolerates partial shade. The potting mix should be evenly **moist** and **well drained**; this plant doesn't like wet soil, but doesn't like to dry out completely either. Fertilize no more than once a month during the growing season with quarter-strength fertilizer. This tender shrub must be moved indoors in winter and kept in the brightest location available.

Tips

Rosemary can be grown in a container as a specimen or with other plants. Low-growing, spreading plants can be grown in hanging baskets. Rosemary can be clipped into balls or cone shapes and grown in an urn-type container for a formal, classic look.

R. officinalis 'Prostratus'

Recommended

R. officinalis is a dense, bushy, evergreen shrub with narrow, dark green leaves. The habit varies somewhat among cultivars from strongly upright to prostrate and spreading. Flowers are usually in shades of blue, but pink-flowered cultivars are available.

To keep plants bushy, pinch the tips back. The bits you pinch off can be used to flavor roast chicken, soups and stews.

Features: evergreen shrub; attractive, fragrant foliage; bright blue, sometimes pink, summer flowers **Height:** 8"–4'
Spread: 1–4' **Hardiness:** zones 8–10; can be overwintered indoors

Rush

Juncus

J. effusus 'Spiralis' with impatiens

Rushes are popular, eye-catching plants, particularly the curly- or spiral-leaved cultivars, which prove fascinating to gardeners and visitors alike.

Growing

Rushes grow well in **full sun** or **partial shade**. The potting mix should be **acidic** and **moist to wet**. Fertilize no more than monthly during the growing season with quarter-strength fertilizer. In winter, move containers to a sheltered location protected from temperature fluctuations where plants are hardy. Grow them as annuals where they aren't hardy.

Tips

Plant rushes in moist containers with other water-loving plants such as iris and sedge. They can even be grown in shallow, gravel-filled water dishes, where they can be used to create a unique, living centerpiece for your patio table.

Recommended

J. effusus (soft rush) forms a tufted clump of long, flexible, stem-like leaves and bears insignificant flowers in summer. The species is rarely grown. **'Spiralis'** (corkscrew rush) forms a tangled mass of curling and corkscrew-like leaves, and cultivars with more corkscrew-like leaves are becoming available. **'Variegated Spiral Rush'** has white-streaked leaves. (Zones 6–8)

J. inflexus (hard rush) forms a clump of stiff, stem-like leaves. **'Afro'** has more tightly spiraled stems than 'Spiralis.'

Features: marginally aquatic perennial; decorative, stem-like leaves **Height:** 18–24"
Spread: 12" **Hardiness:** zones 4–8

Salvia

Salvia

Proven Winners Selection *S. officinalis* 'Purpurea' with African daisy, sedge and others

Spikes of pretty flowers and attractive mounds of foliage help these plants blend into mixed containers.

Growing

Salvias grow best in **full sun** but tolerate light shade. The potting mix should be **humus rich, moist** and **well drained**. Fertilize every two weeks during the growing season with quarter- to half-strength fertilizer. Move containers to a sheltered location protected from temperature fluctuations in winter. Salvias

Sage has been used since at least ancient Greek times as a medicinal and culinary herb.

Also called: sage **Features:** bushy habit; decorative, sometimes fragrant foliage; red, blue, purple, burgundy, lavender, plum, pink, orange, salmon, yellow, cream, white or bicolored, summer flowers **Height:** 12–24" **Spread:** 8–24" **Hardiness:** zones 4–10; tender perennial grown as an annual

S. *splendens* 'Sizzler White' with basil (above)
S. *officinalis* 'Icterina' (below)

are often treated like annuals where they won't survive winter.

Tips

Salvias are attractive plants that combine well with a wide variety of other plants and with each other. Use common sage with other edible herbs such as rosemary, basil and thyme for a fragrant, edible container.

Recommended

S. farinacea (blue sage, mealy cup sage) has bright blue flowers clustered along stems powdered with silver. **'Victoria'** is a popular cultivar with silvery foliage and deep blue flowers. (Zones 8–10)

S. greggii (autumn sage) is a compact, shrubby perennial. It bears red, pink, purple or yellow flowers. **'Raspberry Royale'** bears raspberry red flowers. (Zones 7–9)

S. officinalis is a woody, mounding plant with soft, gray-green leaves. It bears light purple flowers in early and mid-summer. Many attractive cultivars are available, including the silver-leaved **'Berggarten,'** the purple-leaved **'Purpurea,'** the yellow-margined **'Icterina'** and the green and cream variegated **'Tricolor,'** which has a pink flush to the new growth. (Zones 4–8)

S. splendens (salvia, scarlet sage) is a bushy perennial grown as an annual. It bears bright red flowers. Recently, cultivars have become available in white, pink, purple or orange. **'Salsa'** bears solid and bicolored flowers in shades of red, orange, purple, burgundy, cream or pink. **Sizzler Series** bears flowers in burgundy, lavender, pink, plum, red, salmon or white and salmon bicolored.

Scarlet Runner Bean

Phaseolus

Beautiful plants that also provide tasty vegetables are always a welcome addition to the container garden.

Growing

Scarlet runner beans grow best in **full sun**. The potting mix should be **moist** and **well drained**. Fertilize monthly with quarter- to half-strength fertilizer. These beans should be placed near something they can twine around. A porch railing or obelisk is suitable.

Tips

Scarlet runner beans have a carefree habit, twisting and twining around each other and any structure you can provide for them. They are delightful when grown in a container with an obelisk-type frame to climb up. Create a similar look simply by poking three or four long poles into the container and tying them together at the top. Plant these beans in a hanging basket for a unique display.

Recommended

P. coccineus is a twining, annual vine. Scarlet red flowers are borne in clusters in summer, followed by long, edible pods. The edible, dark green pods are tender when young and are best eaten before they become stringy and tough. **Var. *alba*** (Dutch runner bean) bears white flowers. **'Painted Lady'** bears red and white bicolored flowers.

P. coccineus

If you have tall potted lilies, seed scarlet runner bean in the same pot. Once the lilies are done blooming, the tall stems can provide support for the bean as it makes its run upward.

Features: twining vine; red, white or bicolored, summer flowers; edible fruit
Height: 6–8' **Spread:** 1–6'
Hardiness: annual

Sedge

Carex

C. buchananii, from Proven Winners, with argyranthemum and others

Sedges are native to moist wetlands. In the wild, their dense, tufted clumps can mislead hikers into believing the ground is more solid than it is.

Features: tuft-forming, attractive habit; interesting, colorful foliage   **Height:** 1–4'
Spread: 1–4'   **Hardiness:** zones 5–9

With its green, blue, rust, bronze or gold foliage, sedge allows the gardener to add broad, colorful strokes or bright accents to the landscape.

Growing

Sedges grow well in **full sun to partial shade**. The potting mix should be **neutral to slightly alkaline** and **moist to wet**. 'Frosted Curls' is more drought tolerant than other sedges. Fertilize every two weeks during the growing season with quarter-strength fertilizer. Move containers to an unheated shed or garage where they will be protected from temperature fluctuations in winter, or grow them as annuals.

Tips

Sedges offer colorful foliage and rustic texture to contrast with other moisture-loving plants. The cascading habit of many of these grass-like plants makes them an interesting choice to grow as specimens in containers. Space them evenly around your patio or terrace for a formal display. 'Frosted Curls' contrasts well with coarse-textured plants.

Recommended

C. buchananii (leatherleaf sedge) forms a dense clump or tuft of narrow, arching, orange-brown leaves. (Zones 6–9)

C. comans 'Frosted Curls' (New Zealand hair sedge) is a compact, clump-forming, evergreen perennial with fine-textured, pale green, weeping foliage. The foliage appears almost iridescent, with unusual curled and twisted tips. (Zones 7–9)

C. elata 'Aurea' (Bowles' golden sedge) forms a clump of arching, grass-like, yellow leaves with green edges. It bears spikes of tiny, brown or green flowers in early summer.

C. morrowii 'Aureovariegata' (variegated Japanese sedge) forms low tufts of drooping, green-and-yellow-striped foliage. (Zones 6–9)

C. pendula (drooping sedge, weeping sedge) forms a clump of graceful, arching, grass-like, green leaves. Drooping spikes of brown flowers are borne on long stems in late spring and early summer.

C. flagellifera TOFFEE TWIST, a Proven Winners Selection, with petunia, sweet flag and argyranthemum (above), *C. comans* 'Frosted Curls' (below)

Sedum
Sedum

Sedum with sea lavender

$\mathcal{M}$any sedums are grown for their foliage, which can range in color from steel gray-blue and green to red and burgundy. The flowers are an added bonus.

Also called: stonecrop **Features:** mat-forming or upright perennial; yellow, white, red or pink, summer to fall flowers; decorative, fleshy foliage **Height:** 2–24"
Spread: 12–24" **Hardiness:** zones 3–9

Growing
Sedums prefer **full sun** but tolerate partial shade. The potting mix should be **neutral to alkaline** and **very well drained**. West of the Cascades where rain can be plentiful, add perlite or sand to the potting soil and elevate the pots slightly by sitting them on pot feet. Fertilize no more than once a month during the growing season with half-strength fertilizer. Move containers to a sheltered location protected from temperature fluctuations in winter.

Tips
Low-growing sedums make wonderful filler plants for mixed containers, where many of them will grow over the edge of the pot. They can also be grown in low, wide dishes to be placed on a stairway so that they cascade over the edge of the dish and down the stairs. Taller selections make good contrast plants for mixed containers.

Recommended
S. acre (gold moss stonecrop) is a low-growing, wide-spreading plant that bears small, yellow-green flowers.

S. 'Autumn Joy' is a popular upright hybrid. The flowers open pink or red and later fade to deep bronze.

S. spectabile (showy stonecrop) is an upright species with pink flowers. Cultivars are available.

S. spurium (two-row stonecrop) forms a low, wide mat of foliage with deep pink or white flowers. Many cultivars are available and are often grown for their colorful foliage.

Serviceberry

Amelanchier

The *Amelanchier* species are first-rate North American natives, bearing lacy, white flowers in spring, followed by edible berries. In fall, the foliage color ranges from glowing apricot to deep red.

Growing

Serviceberries grow well in **full sun** or **light shade**. The potting mix should be **acidic, humus rich, moist** and **well drained**. Fertilize every two weeks during the growing season with quarter-strength fertilizer. Move containers to a sheltered location protected from temperature fluctuations in winter.

Tips

With spring flowers, edible fruit, attractive leaves that turn red in fall and often artistic branch growth, serviceberries make beautiful specimen plants or even small shade trees for large containers.

Recommended

A. alnifolia (Pacific serviceberry) is a large, rounded, suckering, native shrub that bears clusters of white flowers in late spring and edible, dark purple fruit in summer. Shades of yellow, orange and red color the fall foliage. **'Regent'** is a compact selection that grows 4–6' tall and wide.

A. canadensis (shadblow serviceberry) is a large, upright, suckering shrub. White, spring flowers are followed by edible, purple, summer fruit. The leaves turn orange, scarlet and red in fall.

A. canadensis

Serviceberry fruit can be used in place of blueberries in any recipe, having a similar but generally sweeter flavor.

Also called: saskatoon, juneberry, billberry
Features: single- or multi-stemmed, deciduous large shrub or small tree; spring or early-summer flowers; edible fruit; fall color; habit; bark **Height:** 4–15' **Spread:** 4–15'
Hardiness: zones 3–9

Snapdragon
Antirrhinum

A. *majus* cultivar

Snapdragons are interesting and long-lasting in fresh flower arrangements. The buds continue to mature and open long after the spike has been cut.

Features: clump-forming habit; white, cream, yellow, orange, red, maroon, pink, purple or bicolored, summer flowers; glossy, green through bronze foliage   **Height:** 6"–4'
Spread: 6–12"   **Hardiness:** tender perennial grown as an annual

Gardeners of all ages love the magic of these flowers, which look like delightful, tiny dragon heads.

Growing
Snapdragons prefer **full sun** but tolerate light shade or partial shade. The potting mix should be **humus rich, neutral to alkaline** and **well drained**. Fertilize every two weeks with quarter- to half-strength fertilizer. To encourage bushier growth, pinch the tips of young plants.

Cut off the flower spikes as they fade to promote further blooming.

Tips

Snapdragons are bushy plants of variable height that look lovely planted alone or in mixed containers. There is even a trailing variety that does well in hanging baskets. The strong, upright, vividly colored flower spikes contrast beautifully with arching grasses and broad, leafy plants.

Recommended

A. majus is a bushy, clump-forming plant from which flower spikes emerge in summer. Many cultivars are available in dwarf (up to 12" tall), medium (12–24" tall) and giant (up to 4' tall) sizes. **'Floral Showers'** grows 6–8" tall and bears flowers in a wide range of solid colors and bicolors. **'Lampion'** has a trailing habit and cascades up to 36", making it a great plant for hanging baskets. **'Black Prince'** grows 18" tall and bears striking, dark purple-red flowers set against bronzy green foliage. **Rocket Series** cultivars have good heat tolerance, grow to 4' tall and produce long spikes of brightly colored flowers in many shades. This series does especially well in eastern Washington and Oregon.

A. majus cultivar (above & below)

The genus name Antirrhinum *comes from the Greek language.* Anti *means "against" and* rhis *translates as "snout," referring to the shape of the flower.*

Snow-in-Summer
Cerastium

C. tomentosum

This Mediterranean native looks lovely spilling over the edge of a decorative terra-cotta container.

Features: low, spreading perennial; silvery foliage; white, late-spring flowers
Height: 2–12"   **Spread:** 36" or more
Hardiness: zones 1–8

Snow-in-summer is a tough-as-nails plant that thrives even when neglected.

Growing
Snow-in-summer grows well in **full sun** or **partial shade**. The potting mix should be **well drained**. Fertilize no more than monthly during the growing season with quarter-strength fertilizer. Trim plants back after flowering is complete to encourage new growth and to keep plants looking tidy. Snow-in-summer will suffer in humid heat and in poorly drained soils. Move containers to a sheltered location protected from temperature fluctuations in winter.

Tips
Many gardeners have shied away from this potentially invasive plant, but it is this very quality that makes it a great container plant. It can only spread as far as the pot allows, and it is hardy and attractive. When using it in a mixed container, be sure to use it with other vigorous plants. It makes a good choice for planting beneath a shrub or tree in a large container. Pair it up with some dark-leaved sedums, and you'll have a mixed container planting that won't miss your watering can if you go on vacation.

Recommended
*C. **tomentosum*** forms a low mat of silvery gray foliage and bears white flowers in late spring.

Spider Plant
Chlorophytum

The grass-like, narrow leaf blades arch gracefully as they grow. The long, trailing stems cascade over the pot's edge and carry small plantlets that resemble baby spiders dangling from a silky thread.

Growing

Spider plants grow best in **light shade** or **partial shade** with protection from the hot afternoon sun. The potting mix should be **moist** and **well drained**. Plants are fairly drought tolerant. Fertilize every two weeks during the growing season with quarter-strength fertilizer. Plants can be moved indoors in winter, but it is often easier to snip off a few of the baby plantlets to grow over winter for use the following spring.

Tips

Spider plants make good filler plants for mixed containers. They grow quickly and produce flowers and stems of little plantlets while still quite young. The green or variegated leaves will brighten up a container shared with darker-leaved plants.

Recommended

C. comosum forms a clump of graceful, arching, grass-like leaves. Flowering stems emerge from the rosette bearing tiny, white flowers and young plantlets. The stems are pendant, weighed down by the plantlets. **'Milky Way'** has creamy leaf margins. **'Variegatum'** has cream to white leaf margins. **'Vittatum'** has leaves with a white central stripe and green margins.

C. comosum and *C. comosum* 'Vittatum'

Spider plants are incredibly adaptable, tolerating a wide range of conditions including heat or cold, sun or shade and humid or dry air. They are good choices for balconies and roof gardens because they can handle the wind.

Features: clump-forming habit; decorative, arching, strap-like foliage; stems of trailing or dangling plantlets **Height:** 12" **Spread:** 24–36" **Hardiness:** tender perennial grown as an annual or overwintered indoors

Spruce
Picea

P. glauca var. albertiana 'Conica'

Spruces frequently produce branch mutations, and it is often from these that the dwarf selections are developed.

Features: conical or columnar, evergreen tree or shrub; attractive foliage; varied habit
Height: 2–6' **Spread:** 2–4'
Hardiness: zones 2–8

With a varied selection of small spruce available in a variety of intriguing habits, they are worthy evergreens for the container garden.

Growing
Spruce trees grow best in **full sun**. The potting mix should be **neutral to acidic, moist** and **well drained**. Plant them in the biggest container you can so they won't tip over. Fertilize monthly during the growing season with quarter-strength fertilizer. Spray plants with a strong jet of water to keep them free of spider mites, especially in hot summer areas east of the Cascades. Move containers to a sheltered location protected from the sun and wind in winter. They should be moved into the garden after three to five years.

Tips
Dwarf and slow-growing spruce cultivars are used as specimens in containers. Plant them with drought-tolerant plants in mixed containers, because spruces will quickly consume the available moisture.

Recommended
P. abies (Norway spruce) has many dwarf cultivars. **'Little Gem'** is a slow-growing, rounded cultivar. **'Nidiformis'** (nest spruce) is a slow-growing, low, compact, mounding plant. **Forma *pendula*** are variable, weeping or prostrate forms of spruce. Staked at about 4', they develop into beautiful weeping specimens.

P. glauca **var.** *albertiana* **'Conica'** (dwarf Alberta spruce) is a slow-growing, dense, conical, bushy shrub. Its needles may scorch in too windy or hot a location. **'Jean's Dilly'** is a smaller selection with shorter, thinner needles and twisted branch ends.

Swan River Daisy
Brachyscome (Brachycome)

B. iberidifolia BLUE ZEPHYR

This plant's dainty, daisy-like flowers and lacy, fern-like foliage make a winning combination.

Growing

Swan River daisy prefers **full sun** but benefits from light shade in the afternoon. The potting mix should be **well drained**. Allow the soil to dry between waterings. Fertilize once a month with half-strength fertilizer. Plant out early because cool spring weather encourages compact, sturdy growth. This plant tends to die back when summer gets too hot. If it begins to fade, cut it back and move it to a slightly shadier spot.

Tips

This versatile plant works well in mixed containers and hanging baskets. Plant it near the edges so that the bushy growth will hang out over the sides of the pot and the little flowers will poke through the leaves of its neighbors.

Recommended

B. iberidifolia bears blue-purple or pink-purple, daisy-like flowers all summer. BLUE ZEPHYR, a Proven Selection from Proven Winners, is a heat-tolerant cultivar that will bloom all season. **'Hot Candy'** bears heat-tolerant, dark pink flowers that fade to pale pink.

Deadhead often, and remember to cut off the stem as well as the spent flower.

Features: bushy, mounding or spreading habit; blue, pink, white or purple, summer flowers, usually with yellow centers; feathery foliage **Height:** 6–18" **Spread:** 8–24" **Hardiness:** frost-tolerant annual

Sweet Alyssum
Lobularia

L. maritima with pineapple lily

Leave sweet alyssum out all winter. In spring, remove the previous year's growth to expose the self-sown seedlings below.

Features: fragrant flowers in pink, purple, yellow, salmon and white **Height:** 3–12" **Spread:** 6–24" **Hardiness:** annual

Sweet alyssum is an excellent plant for softening the edges of container plantings and should not be ignored when planting a fragrance garden. Just a few plants are enough to fill your your garden with their sweet, honey-like fragrance.

Growing
Sweet alyssum prefers **full sun** but tolerates light shade. The potting mix should be **well drained** and **moist**. Fertilize monthly with quarter- to half-strength fertilizer. Sweet alyssum may die back a bit during hot and humid summers. Trim it back and ensure the potting mix remains moist to encourage new growth and more flowers when the weather cools.

Tips
Sweet alyssum is good for filling in spaces between taller plants in mixed containers. It will self-seed, sometimes quite a bit, and you may have seedlings popping up in other containers and odd areas in your garden and landscape.

Recommended
L. maritima forms a low, spreading mound of foliage. The entire plant appears to be covered in tiny blossoms when in full flower. Cultivars are available in a range of flower colors. The white varieties are the most fragrant.

Sweet Flag
Acorus

Sweet flags have glossy, often striped leaves that create an attractive display in a mixed container of moisture-loving plants.

Growing

Sweet flags grow best in **full sun**. The potting mix should be **moist to wet**. Fertilize monthly during the growing season with quarter- to half-strength fertilizer. Move containers to a sheltered location such as an unheated shed or garage in winter.

Tips

These plants are much admired for their habit as well as for the wonderful, spicy fragrance of the crushed leaves. Include sweet flags in a mixed container with plants such as calla lilies and elephant ears for a texturally intriguing, moisture loving container.

Recommended

A. calamus (sweet flag) is a large, clump-forming plant with long, narrow, bright green, fragrant foliage. **'Variegatus'** has vertically striped yellow, cream and green leaves.

A. gramineus (dwarf sweet flag, Japanese rush) forms low, fan-shaped clumps of fragrant, glossy, green, narrow leaves. **'Minimus Aureus'** is a very low-growing cultivar with bright golden yellow leaves. **'Ogon,'** a Proven Selection from Proven Winners, has cream-and-green-striped leaves. **'Pusillus'** (dwarf Japanese rush) is a very low-growing cultivar. (Zones 5–11)

Sweet flag was a popular moat-side plant in the past.

A. gramineus 'Ogon'

Features: clump-forming perennial; narrow, stiff or arching, grass-like, sometimes variegated leaves; moisture loving
Height: 4"–5' **Spread:** 4–24"
Hardiness: zones 4–11

Sweet Potato Vine
Ipomoea

I. batatas BLACK HEART, from Proven Winners

The morning glories listed here are not related to the noxious weed called morning glory (Convolvulus arvensis) and will not persist in the garden.

Features: twining climber; white, blue, pink or purple flowers; sometimes variegated or colorful foliage **Height:** 1–10' **Spread:** 12–24" **Hardiness:** annual; tender perennial grown as an annual

This genus offers vigorous vines that look stunning spilling over the edges of mixed containers.

Growing

All *Ipomoea* species grow well in **full sun**. The potting mix should be **light** and **well drained**. Fertilize sweet potato vine once a month with quarter- to half-strength fertilizer. Other ipomoeas will bloom poorly if over-fertilized.

Tips

Sweet potato vines make excellent filler and accent plants in planters and hanging baskets. Sweet potato vines have colorful foliage, and morning glories and moonflowers have lovely, trumpet-shaped flowers. The climbing vines will grow up small trellises or other structures. Grow moonflower on a porch or on a trellis near a patio that is used in the evenings so that the sweetly scented flowers can be fully enjoyed.

Recommended

I. alba (moonflower) is a twining, perennial climber with heart-shaped leaves and sweetly scented, white flowers that open only at night.

I. batatas (sweet potato vine) is a twining, perennial climber that is usually treated as a bushy or trailing plant rather than a climber. It is grown for its attractive foliage rather than its flowers. Cultivars with different foliage color variations are available. BLACK HEART, a Proven Selection by Proven Winners, has heart-shaped, dark purple foliage. 'Blackie' has dark purple (almost black), deeply lobed leaves. 'Margarita' has yellow-green foliage on a fairly compact plant. 'Tricolor' is a compact plant with light green, cream and bright pink variegated leaves.

I. purpurea (morning glory) is a twining, annual climber with heart-shaped leaves and trumpet-shaped, purple, pink, blue or white flowers.

I. tricolor (morning glory) is a twining, annual climber with heart-shaped, purple or blue flowers with white throats. There are several cultivars, including the popular 'Heavenly Blue,' which has sky blue flowers with white centers.

I. batatas 'Margarita' with coleus, English ivy, lamium and others (above), *I. batatas* 'Margarita' with juniper, coral bells and bamboo grass (below)

Thyme
Thymus

T. x citriodorus 'Golden King' with parsley, rosemary and others

In the Middle Ages, it was believed that drinking a thyme infusion would enable one to see fairies.

Features: mounding or creeping perennial; purple, pink or white, late-spring to early-summer flowers; tiny, fuzzy or glossy, often fragrant foliage **Height:** 2–18"
Spread: 4–16" **Hardiness:** zones 3–9

pright or creeping, thyme is an excellent plant for a container garden. Its tiny flowers attract a variety of pollinators.

Growing
Thyme prefers **full sun**. The potting mix should be **humus rich** and **very well drained**. Mix in compost or earthworm castings. These plants are fairly drought tolerant. Fertilize no more than monthly during the growing season with quarter-strength fertilizer. Move containers to a sheltered location protected from temperature fluctuations in winter.

Tips
Thyme is a nice addition to your herb collection, growing nicely by itself or mixed with other herbs. It can also be used at the edge of a mixed container, where the tiny leaves will soften the appearance of coarser-leaved companions.

Recommended
T. citriodorus (lemon-scented thyme) forms a tidy, rounded mound of lemon-scented foliage and pale pink flowers. '**Argenteus**' has silver-edged leaves. '**Golden King**' has yellow-margined leaves. (Zones 5–9)

T. serpyllum (mother of thyme, wild thyme) is a low, creeping, mat-forming plant. It bears purple flowers. '**Elfin**' forms tiny, dense mounds of foliage. It rarely flowers. '**Minimalist**' ('Minimus') is lower growing than the species and bears pink flowers. '**Snowdrift**' has white flowers.

T. vulgaris (common thyme) forms a bushy mound of dark green leaves. The flowers may be purple, pink or white. '**Silver Posie**' has pale pink flowers and silver-edged leaves. (Zones 4–9)

Tradescantia
Tradescantia

Often reserved for hanging baskets, these plants create a stunning display of arching foliage that looks lovely in a tall, urn-shaped planter.

Growing

Tradescantias grow well in **full sun** or **partial shade**. The potting mix should be **moist** and **well drained**. Fertilize every two weeks during the growing season with quarter- to half-strength fertilizer. Move containers to a sheltered location protected from temperature fluctuations in winter. Tender plants will have to be brought indoors before the first frost or replaced the following summer.

Tips

Tradescantias make good hanging-basket plants and can be grown alone or with other trailing plants. In containers, they make attractive companions for coarse-textured and upright-growing plants.

Recommended

T. andersoniana (spiderwort) forms a clump of stems and arching, strap-like foliage. Clusters of blue, purple, pink, red or white flowers are produced from early summer to fall. **'Concord Grape'** has silvery blue-green foliage and dark purple flowers. **'Little Doll'** is a dwarf selection that bears light blue flowers.

T. pallida 'Purpurea' ('Purple Heart') is a tender, trailing or mound-forming plant with purple stems and bronzy purple leaves. It bears pink flowers in summer. This plant is drought tolerant.

T. pallida 'Purpurea' is a tender perennial and must be moved indoors to a bright location if you wish to overwinter it.

T. x *andersoniana* cultivar with golden hakone grass, begonia, hosta and others (above), *T.* x *andersoniana* 'Sweet Kate,' from Proven Winners (below)

Features: clump-forming, mound-forming or trailing habit; colorful foliage; attractive, pink, blue, purple, red or white, summer flowers
Height: 8–24"   **Spread:** 12–24"
Hardiness: zones 3–9; tender perennial grown as an annual

Tulip
Tulipa

T. hybrid

Tulips are a welcome sight as we enjoy the warm days of spring.

Growing

Tulips grow best in **full sun**. The flowers tend to bend toward the light in partial or light shade. Shorter tulip varieties, such as *T. fosteriana,* and the rock garden tulips do best in pots that don't get full sun. The potting mix should be **well drained**. Plant bulbs in fall and keep containers in a sheltered location. Plant bulbs that have been cold treated in spring. Fertilize with quarter-strength fertilizer every two weeks as flowering finishes and until the foliage begins to fade if you are planning to keep your bulbs for fall planting or storing over the winter.

When your tulips are done blooming, you can either dig them from the pot and add summer annuals, or just cut them to the ground and plant right on top of the bulbs. Tulips don't bloom as well the second year in pots, so treat them as annuals or remove them from the pots and replant into the ground after they bloom the first year.

Tips

Tulips provide the best display when planted in groups in mixed or solo containers. Plant them with other spring-blooming plants such as pansies and primroses for a pretty display that welcomes the approaching summer.

Recommended

There are about 100 species of tulips and thousands of hybrids and cultivars. They come in dozens of shades except blue, with many bicolored or multi-colored varieties. Check with your local garden center in early fall for the best selection.

Features: perennial bulb; spring flowers
Height: 6–30"   **Spread:** 2–8"
Hardiness: zones 3–8

Verbena
Verbena

Verbena is an outstanding container and hanging-basket plant. The trailing stems poke brightly colored flower clusters out in unexpected places.

Growing

Verbenas grow best in **full sun**. The potting mix should be **very well drained**. Fertilize every two weeks in summer with half-strength fertilizer. Pinch young plants back to encourage bushy growth. Verbenas will overwinter in containers in the mild areas of western Washington and Oregon if placed in a protected location out of the winter rains.

Tips

Use verbenas in mixed containers, hanging baskets and window boxes. They are good substitutes for ivy geraniums where the sun is hot and where a roof overhang keeps these mildew-prone plants dry.

Recommended

V. x *hybrida* is a bushy plant that may be upright or spreading. It bears clusters of small flowers in shades of white, purple, blue, pink, red, salmon, coral or yellow. **Babylon Series** is a group of compact, bushy plants with flowers in shades of deep or light blue, bright or light pink, dark or light purple, red or white. **'Peaches and Cream'** is a spreading plant with flowers that open soft peachy pink and fade to white. SUPERBENA SERIES, from Proven Winners, is a group of mounding then cascading, mildew-resistant plants with large, vividly colored flowers in shades of purple, burgundy, coral, red, pink or blue.

V. SUPERBENA DARK BLUE with salvia and euphorbia

To rejuvenate foliage and encourage more blooms, cut back the plants by half in mid-summer.

Features: mounding to cascading habit; flowers in shades of red, pink, purple, blue or white, sometimes with white centers
Height: 8–24"　**Spread:** 12–24"
Hardiness: tender perennial grown as an annual

Vinca

Vinca

V. minor and *V. minor* 'Illumination' with geraniums

With glossy, deep green leaves and periwinkle blue flowers, vinca has an attractive presence in the container garden. This evergreen plant will provide you with color during the chilly, gray days of winter.

Growing

Grow vinca in **partial to full shade**. The potting mix should be evenly **moist** and **well drained**. Fertilize monthly during the growing season with quarter-strength fertilizer. Move containers to a sheltered location out of the wind in winter.

Also called: periwinkle **Features:** low, trailing, hardy or tender vine; blue-purple, pale blue, reddish purple or white, mid-spring to fall flowers; green or variegated, glossy foliage **Height:** 4–12" **Spread:** 2–4' **Hardiness:** zones 3–9

Tips

Vinca is a useful, attractive filler plant for containers and hanging baskets. Poke a few rooted stems in here and there to provide a dark green background in your mixed containers.

Recommended

V. major (greater periwinkle) forms a low mat of trailing stems with glossy, dark green leaves. It bears purple or blue flowers from spring to fall. It is often grown as an annual. **'Variegata'** has irregular, creamy margins on light green, glossy leaves. (Zones 6–9)

V. minor (lesser periwinkle) forms a low, loose mat of trailing stems. Purple or blue flowers are borne in spring and sporadically all summer. **'Atropurpurea'** bears reddish purple flowers. **'Illumination'** has vivid gold foliage marked with green patches.

Weigela

Weigela

W. florida FINE WINE, a Proven Winners Color Choice Selection

Weigelas have been improved through breeding, and specimens with more compact forms, longer flowering periods and greater cold tolerance are now available.

Growing

Weigelas prefer **full sun** but tolerate partial shade. The potting mix should be **well drained**. Fertilize monthly during the growing season with half-strength fertilizer. Move containers to a sheltered location protected from temperature fluctuations in winter.

Tips

With their attractive foliage and long flowering period, weigelas are great as focal points alone or in mixed containers. Combine a purple-leaved weigela with a silver-leaved, white-flowered, trailing plant such as snow-in-summer to soften the edges of the container and to create a lovely contrast.

Recommended

W. florida is a bushy, spreading shrub with arching branches that bears clusters of dark pink flowers. Many hybrids and cultivars are available. CARNAVAL bears red, white or pink flowers. FINE WINE is a compact selection of WINE & ROSES with good branching, dark burgundy foliage and hot pink flowers. MIDNIGHT WINE is a low, mounding dwarf with dark burgundy foliage. **'Polka'** has bright pink flowers. **'Red Prince'** produces dark red flowers. **'Rubidor'** has yellow foliage and red flowers. **'Variegata'** has yellow and green variegated foliage and pink flowers. WINE & ROSES has dark burgundy foliage and rosy pink flowers.

Weigela will become too large for a container after three to five years and should be moved to the garden when it does.

Features: upright or low, spreading, deciduous shrub; attractive, late-spring, early-summer and, sporadically, fall flowers; green, bronze or purple foliage
Height: 1–6'   **Spread:** 1–4'
Hardiness: zones 3–8

Yarrow
Achillea

A. millefolium 'Terra Cotta'

Yarrow will happily self-seed, eventually turning up in most of your containers and anywhere else the seeds happen to land.

Features: clump-forming perennial; white, yellow, red, orange, pink or purple, mid-summer to early-fall flowers; attractive foliage; spreading habit   **Height:** 4"–4'
Spread: 12–36"   **Hardiness:** zones 2–8

arrows are informal, tough plants with a fantastic color range.

Growing
Yarrows grow best in **full sun**. The potting mix should be **light** and **well drained**. These plants tolerate drought. Fertilize no more than monthly during the growing season with quarter-strength fertilizer. Too much fertilizer results in weak, floppy growth. Deadhead to prolong blooming. Move containers to a sheltered location protected from temperature fluctuations in winter.

Tips
Yarrow thrives in hot, dry locations where nothing else will grow. If you often forget to water, yarrow could be the plant for you. Combine it with other drought-tolerant plants such as sedum and hens and chicks. The fine, ferny foliage of yarrow will contrast with the coarse, fleshy foliage of the other two plants.

Recommended
A. millefolium (common yarrow) forms a clump of soft, finely divided foliage and bears white flowers. Many cultivars exist, with flowers in a wide range of colors. '**Apple Blossom**' has light pink flowers. '**Paprika**' bears yellow-centered, red flowers that fade to pink, yellow or cream. '**Summer Pastels**' bears white, pink, yellow, purple and sometimes red or salmon-colored flowers. '**Terra Cotta**' has orange-red flowers that fade to light rusty orange or creamy orange.

Yew

Taxus

Yews are among the only reliable evergreens for full sun and deep shade.

Growing

Yews grow well in any light conditions from **full sun to full shade**. The potting mix should be **moist** and **well drained**. Fertilize monthly during the growing season with half-strength fertilizer. Move them to a sheltered location out of the wind and sun in winter.

Tips

Yews are often used to create topiary specimens and can be clipped to maintain a small, neat form for a container. Specimens can be planted alone or used with annuals and perennials for a mixed display.

Male and female flowers are borne on separate plants. Both must be present for the attractive red seed cups to form.

Recommended

T. x media (English-Japanese yew), a cross between *T. baccata* (English yew) and *T. cuspidata* (Japanese yew), has the vigor of English yew and the cold hardiness of Japanese yew. It forms a rounded, upright tree or shrub, though the size and form can vary among the many cultivars. **'Brownii'** is a dense, rounded cultivar. **'Hicksii'** is a narrow, columnar form. **'Tautonii'** is a slow-growing, rounded, spreading cultivar.

These trees tolerate windy, dry and polluted conditions but dislike excessive heat, and on the hotter south or southwest side of a building, they may suffer needle scorch.

T. x media 'Sunburst' (above)
T. x media 'Densiformis' (below)

Features: conical, columnar, bushy or spreading, evergreen tree or shrub; attractive foliage; red fruit **Height:** 1–10'
Spread: 1–5' **Hardiness:** zones 4–7

Yucca
Yucca

Y. filamentosa with maidenhair vine, African daisy, vinca and dracaena

Yucca adds a bold presence and texture to your mixed planters.

Growing
Yucca grows best in **full sun** but tolerates partial shade. The potting mix must

be **well drained**. This plant is very drought tolerant. Fertilize no more than once a month during the growing season with quarter-strength fertilizer. Move it to a sheltered location in winter, or just leave it where it is. If it doesn't make it through winter, simply replace it in spring. Remove spent flower spikes and dead leaves as needed.

Tips
Yucca makes a strong architectural statement and is used as a specimen in planters to give a garden a southern appearance. Combine it with low, soft, trailing plants to create some contrast.

Yuccas are perfect for urns because many urn-shaped containers have so little room for soil that they dry out quickly. Yuccas also grow in a natural symmetrical shape, giving them a formal look for classic gardens.

Recommended
Y. filamentosa has long, stiff, finely serrated, pointed leaves with threads that peel back from the edges. It is the most frost-hardy species available. **'Bright Edge'** has leaves with yellow margins. **'Golden Sword'** has leaves with yellow centers and green margins. **'Hofer's Blue'** has attractive, blue-green leaves and is salt tolerant.

Also called: Adam's needle
Features: stiff, rosette-forming, evergreen perennial; white or creamy, summer flowers; stiff, decorative foliage **Height:** 24–36"; up to 6' in flower **Spread:** 24–36"
Hardiness: zones 5–10

Glossary

Acidic soil: soil with a pH lower than 7.0

Annual: a plant that germinates, flowers, sets seed and dies in one growing season

Alkaline soil: soil with a pH higher than 7.0

Basal foliage: leaves that form from the crown, at the base of the plant

Bract: a modified leaf at the base of a flower or flower cluster

Corm: a bulb-like, food-storing, underground stem, resembling a bulb without scales

Crown: the part of the plant at or just below soil level where the shoots join the roots

Cultivar: a cultivated plant variety with one or more distinct differences from the species, e.g., in flower color or disease resistance

Deadhead: to remove spent flowers to maintain a neat appearance and encourage a longer blooming season

Direct sow: to sow seeds directly in the garden

Dormancy: a period of plant inactivity, usually during winter or unfavorable conditions

Double flower: a flower with an unusually large number of petals

Espalier: a tree trained from a young age to grow on a single plane

Genus: a category of biological classification between the species and family levels; the first word in a scientific name indicates the genus

Grafting: a type of propagation in which a stem or bud of one plant is joined onto the rootstock of another plant of a closely related species

Hardy: capable of surviving cold weather or frost without protection

Hip: the fruit of a rose, containing the seeds

Humus: decomposed or decomposing organic material in the soil

Hybrid: a plant resulting from natural or human-induced cross-breeding between varieties, species or genera

Neutral soil: soil with a pH of 7.0

Offset: a horizontal branch that forms at the base of a plant and produces new plants from buds at its tips

Panicle: a compound flower structure with groups of flowers on short stalks

Perennial: a plant that takes three or more years to complete its life cycle

pH: a measure of acidity or alkalinity

Rhizome: a root-like, food-storing stem that grows horizontally at or just below soil level, from which new shoots may emerge

Rootball: the root mass and surrounding soil of a plant

Seedhead: dried, inedible fruit that contains seeds; the fruiting stage of the inflourescence

Self-seeding: reproducing by means of seeds without human assistance, so that new plants constantly replace those that die

Semi-double flower: a flower with petals in two or three rings

Single flower: a flower with a single ring of typically four or five petals

Species: the fundamental unit of biological classification; the entity from which cultivars and varieties are derived

Standard: a shrub or small tree grown with an erect main stem, accomplished either through pruning and training or by grafting the plant onto a tall, straight stock

Sucker: a shoot that comes up from the root, often some distance from the plant; it can be separated to form a new plant once it develops its own roots

Tender: incapable of surviving the climatic conditions of a given region and requiring protection from frost or cold

Tuber: the thick section of a rhizome bearing nodes and buds

Variegation: foliage that has more than one color, often patched or striped or bearing leaf margins of a different color

Variety: a naturally occurring variant of a species

SPECIES by Common Name

Species by Common Name	LIGHT				SOIL MIX		FEATURES						
	Full Sun	Light Shade	Partial Shade	Full Shade	Soil-based	Soil-less	Variegated	Flowers	Foliage	Fruit/Seed	Scent	Specimen	Grouping
African Daisy	•					•		•					•
Agapanthus	•	•	•			•		•	•				•
Angel's Trumpet	•					•		•	•		•	•	
Arborvitae	•	•	•		•	•	•		•			•	
Argyranthemum	•					•		•	•				•
Asparagus Fern		•	•			•			•				
Bacopa			•			•		•	•				
Basil	•					•			•		•		
Bay Laurel	•	•	•		•	•			•			•	
Begonia		•	•			•		•	•				•
Bidens	•					•		•	•				
Black-eyed Susan	•		•			•		•					•
Black-eyed Susan Vine	•	•	•			•		•	•				
Blood Grass	•		•			•			•				
Blue Fescue	•		•			•			•				
Blue Oat Grass	•					•			•				
Bougainvillea	•					•	•	•	•				
Bugleweed		•	•			•	•	•	•				
Calla Lily	•					•		•	•			•	
Canna Lily	•					•	•	•	•			•	
Catch-Fly	•	•				•		•					
Cilantro/Coriander	•					•		•	•	•			
Clematis	•					•		•	•				•
Cleome	•					•		•	•		•	•	
Clover	•		•			•	•	•	•				
Coleus		•	•			•	•		•				•
Coral Bells		•	•			•	•	•	•				•
Croscosmia	•					•		•	•			•	
Cuphea	•		•			•		•					
Dahlia	•					•		•	•			•	
Daylily	•	•	•	•		•		•	•			•	•
Dogwood	•	•	•	•	•	•	•	•	•	•		•	
Dusty Miller	•								•				•

Moist	Well-drained	Dry	Fertile	Average	Poor	Upright	Bushy	Climber/Trailer	Architectural	Page Number	SPECIES by Common Name
•	•		•	•		•	•			62	African Daisy
•	•		•						•	63	Agapanthus
•	•		•	•		•	•		•	65	Angel's Trumpet
•	•			•	•	•	•			66	Arborvitae
	•			•			•			68	Argyranthemum
•				•			•	•		69	Asparagus Fern
•	•			•				•		70	Bacopa
•	•		•	•			•			71	Basil
•	•			•		•	•			72	Bay Laurel
	•		•	•			•	•		73	Begonia
•	•		•	•			•			75	Bidens
•	•	•		•		•				76	Black-eyed Susan
•	•		•	•				•		78	Black-eyed Susan Vine
•	•			•					•	79	Blood Grass
•	•			•					•	80	Blue Fescue
	•				•				•	81	Blue Oat Grass
•	•		•	•		•	•	•		82	Bougainvillea
	•			•			•	•		83	Bugleweed
•	•		•	•		•			•	84	Calla Lily
•	•		•	•		•			•	86	Canna Lily
•	•		•	•		•	•			87	Catch-Fly
	•			•		•				88	Cilantro/Coriander
•	•		•	•		•	•	•		89	Clematis
•	•			•	•	•	•			91	Cleome
•	•			•	•		•			92	Clover
•	•		•	•			•			93	Coleus
•	•			•			•			95	Coral Bells
•	•			•					•	97	Crocosmia
•	•			•		•	•			98	Cuphea
•	•		•	•		•	•			99	Dahlia
•	•			•					•	101	Daylily
	•			•		•	•			102	Dogwood
	•			•	•		•			104	Dusty Miller

SPECIES
by Common Name

	LIGHT				SOIL MIX		FEATURES						
	Full Sun	Light Shade	Partial Shade	Full Shade	Soil-based	Soil-less	Variegated	Flowers	Foliage	Fruit/Seed	Scent	Specimen	Grouping
Dwarf Morning Glory	•					•		•					
Elder	•		•		•	•	•	•	•	•		•	
Elephant Ears		•		•		•			•			•	
Euonymus	•				•	•	•		•			•	
Euphorbia	•	•				•		•	•			•	
False Cypress	•				•	•			•	•		•	
Fan Flower	•	•				•		•					
Flowering Maple	•	•				•	•	•	•			•	
Foamflower		•	•	•		•	•	•	•				•
Fothergilla	•	•	•		•	•		•	•		•	•	
Fuchsia		•	•			•		•	•				
Geranium	•					•	•	•	•		•		•
Glory Bush	•					•		•	•			•	
Golden Hakone Grass		•	•			•	•		•				•
Golden Marguerite	•					•		•	•				•
Hardy Geranium		•	•			•		•	•				
Hebe	•		•		•	•		•	•		•	•	
Heliotrope	•					•		•	•		•		
Hens and Chicks	•		•			•	•	•	•				•
Hosta		•	•				•	•	•		•		
Hydrangea	•		•		•	•		•	•			•	
Hyssop	•		•			•		•	•		•		
Impatiens		•	•			•		•					•
Iris	•					•	•	•	•				
Japanese Painted Fern		•	•	•		•	•		•				
Kalanchoe		•	•			•		•	•				
Lady's Mantle		•	•			•		•	•				
Lamium		•	•			•	•	•	•				
Lavender	•					•		•	•		•		
Licorice Plant	•					•	•		•				
Lilac	•				•	•		•			•	•	
Lilyturf		•	•			•	•	•	•				•
Lobelia	•		•					•					•

Moist	Well-drained	Dry	Fertile	Average	Poor	Upright	Bushy	Climber/Trailer	Architectural	Page Number	SPECIES by Common Name
	•				•		•			105	Dwarf Morning Glory
•	•			•		•	•			106	Elder
•				•		•			•	108	Elephant Ears
•	•			•			•	•		109	Euonymous
•	•				•		•			111	Euphorbia
•	•			•		•	•			113	False Cypress
•	•			•			•	•		115	Fan Flower
•	•		•	•		•				116	Flowering Maple
•	•			•			•			117	Foamflower
•	•			•			•			118	Fothergilla
•	•		•				•	•		119	Fuchsia
	•		•	•			•			121	Geranium
•	•		•	•			•			123	Glory Bush
•	•		•	•				•	•	124	Golden Hakone Grass
	•	•		•	•		•			125	Golden Marguerite
	•			•			•			126	Hardy Geranium
•	•			•			•			128	Hebe
•	•			•			•			130	Heliotrope
	•			•	•					131	Hens and Chicks
•	•			•			•			132	Hosta
•	•			•			•	•		134	Hydrangea
	•			•		•	•			136	Hyssop
•	•			•			•			137	Impatiens
•	•			•		•			•	138	Iris
•				•			•			140	Japanese Painted Fern
	•			•		•	•	•		142	Kalanchoe
•	•			•			•			143	Lady's Mantle
•	•			•	•			•		144	Lamium
	•			•	•	•	•			146	Lavender
	•			•			•	•		147	Licorice Plant
	•			•	•	•	•			148	Lilac
•	•			•	•	•			•	149	Lilyturf
•	•			•		•	•	•		150	Lobelia

SPECIES by Common Name	LIGHT				SOIL MIX		FEATURES						
	Full Sun	Light Shade	Partial Shade	Full Shade	Soil-based	Soil-less	Variegated	Flowers	Foliage	Fruit/Seed	Scent	Specimen	Grouping
Lotus Vine	•		•			•			•				
Lungwort		•	•	•		•	•	•	•				
Lysimachia	•		•			•		•					
Maidenhair Fern		•	•			•			•				•
Maple	•	•			•	•			•			•	
Million Bells	•					•		•					
Mondo Grass	•	•	•			•		•	•				•
Monkey Flower		•	•			•		•					•
Nasturtium	•					•	•	•	•				
Nemesia	•					•		•					
Nicotiana	•	•	•			•		•	•		•		
Oregano	•					•			•		•		
Oxalis	•		•			•		•	•				
Pansy	•					•		•					•
Parsley	•		•			•			•				
Penstemon	•					•		•					
Perilla	•		•			•			•				
Petunia	•					•		•				•	•
Phormium	•					•	•		•			•	
Piggyback Plant		•	•	•		•	•		•			•	
Plectranthus		•	•			•	•		•				
Poor Man's Orchid	•		•			•		•					•
Purple Fountain Grass	•					•		•	•				
Rhododendron/Azalea		•	•		•	•		•	•			•	
Rose	•				•	•		•	•	•	•	•	
Rosemary	•							•	•		•	•	
Rush	•		•			•			•				
Salvia	•					•	•	•	•		•		
Scarlet Runner Bean	•					•		•	•	•			
Sedge	•		•			•			•			•	
Sedum	•					•		•	•				•
Serviceberry	•	•			•	•		•	•	•		•	
Snapdragon	•					•		•	•				•

Moist	Well-drained	Dry	Fertile	Average	Poor	Upright	Bushy	Climber/Trailer	Architectural	Page Number	SPECIES by Common Name
	•			•	•		•	•		152	Lotus Vine
•	•		•	•			•			153	Lungwort
•	•			•	•	•	•	•		154	Lysimachia
•	•			•	•		•			155	Maidenhair Fern
	•			•	•	•	•			156	Maple
•	•		•	•			•	•		158	Million Bells
•	•			•					•	159	Mondo Grass
•			•	•			•	•		160	Monkey Flower
•	•			•	•		•	•		161	Nasturtium
•	•			•			•	•		162	Nemesia
•	•		•	•		•		•		163	Nicotiana
	•			•	•		•			164	Oregano
	•			•			•			165	Oxalis
•	•			•						166	Pansy
•	•			•			•			168	Parsley
	•	•		•	•	•	•			169	Penstemon
•	•		•				•			170	Perilla
	•			•	•		•	•		171	Petunia
•	•			•		•			•	173	Phormium
•	•			•			•	•		174	Piggyback Plant
•	•			•			•	•		175	Plectranthus
•	•		•			•		•		176	Poor Man's Orchid
	•			•	•	•			•	177	Purple Fountain Grass
•	•		•				•			179	Rhododendron/Azalea
•	•		•	•			•			181	Rose
•	•			•	•	•	•	•		183	Rosemary
•				•	•				•	184	Rush
•	•			•			•			185	Salvia
•	•			•				•		187	Scarlet Runner Bean
•				•					•	188	Sedge
	•			•	•	•	•			190	Sedum
•	•			•		•	•			191	Serviceberry
	•		•	•		•	•			192	Snapdragon

SPECIES
by Common Name

SPECIES by Common Name	LIGHT				SOIL MIX		FEATURES						
	Full Sun	Light Shade	Partial Shade	Full Shade	Soil-based	Soil-less	Variegated	Flowers	Foliage	Fruit/Seed	Scent	Specimen	Grouping
Snow-in-Summer	•		•			•		•	•				•
Spider Plant		•	•			•	•		•				
Spruce	•				•	•			•	•		•	
Swan River Daisy	•					•		•	•				•
Sweet Alyssum	•					•			•		•		•
Sweet Flag	•					•	•		•				
Sweet Potato Vine	•					•	•	•	•				
Thyme	•					•	•	•	•		•		
Tradescantia	•		•			•		•	•				•
Tulip	•					•		•					•
Verbena	•					•		•					
Vinca		•	•	•		•	•	•	•				
Weigela	•				•	•	•	•	•			•	
Yarrow	•					•		•	•				
Yew	•	•	•	•	•	•			•	•		•	
Yucca	•					•	•		•			•	

Moist	Well-drained	Dry	Fertile	Average	Poor	Upright	Bushy	Climber/Trailer	Architectural	Page Number	SPECIES by Common Name
	•			•	•					194	Snow-in-Summer
•	•			•			•	•		195	Spider Plant
•	•			•		•	•			196	Spruce
	•			•			•			197	Swan River Daisy
•	•			•			•			198	Sweet Alyssum
•				•		•			•	199	Sweet Flag
	•			•	•			•		200	Sweet Potato Vine
	•			•	•	•	•			202	Thyme
•	•			•			•	•		203	Tradescantia
	•			•		•				204	Tulip
	•		•	•			•	•		205	Verbena
•	•			•				•		206	Vinca
	•			•			•			207	Weigela
	•			•	•		•			208	Yarrow
•	•			•		•	•			209	Yew
	•	•		•	•	•			•	210	Yucca

Index of Recommended Plant Names

Main entries are in **boldface**; botanical names are in *italics*.

About the Authors

Marianne Binetti is a well-known gardening personality whose syndicated garden column reaches over a million readers each week in the *Seattle Post-Intelligencer* and is carried in 20 newspapers across Washington State. She contributes to several national magazines, including *Better Homes and Gardens*, *Woman's Day* and *Flower and Garden*. She has made guest appearances on HGTV, the Discovery Channel and *Gardening in America*, and her light-hearted approach to gardening appeals to TV and radio audiences alike.

Don Williamson has turned his passion for gardening into his life's work. His background is in landscaping, golf course construction and management, and in the design and construction of formal landscape settings. With a degree in Applied Horticultural Technology and professional certificates in Turf Management, he has written and co-written several gardening books.

Alison Beck has been gardening since she was a child. Author of more than two dozen gardening books, she showcases her talent for practical advice and her passion for gardening. Alison has a diploma in Horticultural Technology and a degree in Creative Writing.

Laura Peters is a certified Master Gardener with experience in every aspect of the horticultural industry. A talented garden photographer whose work is featured in many gardening books, she enjoys sharing her practical knowledge of organic gardening, plant varieties and gardening products with fellow gardeners.